A BANK STREET APPROACH

The basic philosophy of The Bank Street College of Education has been described as the "developmental-interaction" approach. "Developmental" refers to the predictable ages and stages of a child's physical, intellectual, and social growth. "Interaction" refers to a child's external relationships with the environment, adults, and other children. It also includes the child's internal interactions, the blending of intellect and emotion.

This approach to education translates from theory to a way of living with children. It applies to home life as well as to school. Indeed, a child's first and most enduring learning begins at home with parents and siblings as the earliest teachers at the child's most impressionable stage. Bank Street's philosophy offers parents and other caring adults a sensitive and sensible approach to helping children explore, discover, and understand their world. It is a way of sharing ideas and extending interests that match the child's abilities and curiosity. It is a framework that supports and values the child's growth toward independence.

Sibling Rivalry explores the vast range of sibling relationships, both positive and negative, in simple, direct language that turns these theories into concrete ideas. This book offers a practical guide for what to expect in sibling behavior, and many options for handling it. With its clear explanations and many lively anecdotes, the book helps parents to view sibling rivalry within the context of the child's total development and the Bank Street philosophy.

Other Books in The Bank Street College of Education
Child Development Series:

Love and Discipline
by Barbara Brenner

Kids and Play
by Joanne F. Oppenheim

Getting Ready to Read
by Betty Doyle Boegehold

SIBLING RIVALRY

Prepared by
THE BANK STREET COLLEGE
of EDUCATION

Seymour V. Reit
AUTHOR

DR. DOROTHY W. GROSS
CONSULTANT

WILLIAM H. HOOKS
SERIES EDITOR

BALLANTINE BOOKS · NEW YORK

B4643049929

Contents

Expanded Contents

CHAPTER 4

Competition—And How to Deal with It

CHAPTER 5

Parents Talk about Competition

CHAPTER 6

—And Baby Makes Four

CHAPTER 7
Parents Talk about the Second Baby

CHAPTER 8
Love Is Not a Cookie Jar

CHAPTER 9
*A Father's Diary: Or, How I Grew Closer to My Daughter
When My Son Was Born*
by James A. Levine

CHAPTER 10
Special Occasions, Special People

CHAPTER 11
Matched Sets

Foreword

I have two memories of the time when my sister, five years younger than myself, joined our family. My first memory, in the hospital, is crowded with excited grown-ups filling and darkening a tiny hallway. There is barely enough room for me, although, at five years old, I reached no higher than anyone's thigh. There is a door with a high window in it. Suddenly, a red, crumple-faced, dark-headed bundle appears in the window, held by an invisible someone. My voice rings out, excited, proud of the cleverness of my observation, "It looks like a monkey!" And the grown-ups shush me in shocked tones.

The other memory is more complex—and needs some history. When mother went to the hospital to give birth to my sister, I was left with my grandparents. During my stay with them, I fell and broke an ankle, which required a stay in the hospital (not the same one as my mother's!) and the wearing of a full cast, thigh to toe.

In this second memory I am in the backseat of a car, with a blanket covering my cast, going to bring my mother and the baby home. My aunt and my grandmother solemnly instruct me not to tell my mother about the cast, because it would upset her. We arrive at the hospital, and my mother, baby in arms, bends into the car with joyful face to greet me. Defying all the family, I throw back the blanket. "Look, Ma!" My mother gasps and as she sags, she almost drops the baby.

The only trouble with these memories is that they couldn't both have happened, my first sight of my baby sister occurring both in the hospital hallway and from the recesses of an automobile. Nor could a child with a broken leg have been outside the nursery exclaiming about monkey resemblances. Why, then, do I tell these tales? Because whatever their relation to objective fact, the memories—and they are vivid and detailed—reflect deeply felt responses to the arrival of a sibling in a family.

First is the theme of rejection of the new baby. This is evident in both memories. In one, she is perceived as ugly and alien, a monkey; and in the other, she is even put in danger, almost caused to fall. Second is the sense of not being seen, perhaps even neglected. This is shown in the shadowed hospital hallway, where the older sister is not even noticed amidst the jostling grown-ups—until she demands attention with a clever comment. Third, what mixed feelings are shown toward the mother! "Look!" says the child. "Look what happened to me when you weren't here! I don't care if you're upset at seeing my cast! You should be! You shouldn't have gone away! Now you can drop that baby (even literally) and take care of *me*!"

As I write this, a follow-up memory arises. We arrive home together, my mother, my new sister, other relatives, and me in my leg cast. The apartment is full of people coming and going. I am in a bed in my parents' room, watching my mother crying and exclaiming over me. I don't understand her being upset, because I love being the center of all the excitement. Now she will pay attention to me!

Many parents with two or more children will recognize the intensely conflicted nature of the feelings I've described (and may remember them from their own childhood): rejection of the baby together with interest in the odd little creature, a sense of invisibility accompanied by determination to get attention, and the combination of need for mother and anger at her. All these, along with the affection and sense of alliance that usually emerge later, are wrapped up in what we call sibling rivalry, a somewhat simple designation for such a highly complex phenomenon.

Indeed, one of the primary themes of this book is that sibling relationships are not simple. How could it be otherwise, when no intimate human relationship is simple? Sound relationships, including those between siblings, involve a rich mix: having one's own needs met and the joy of fulfilling another's, the continuing interest in another person, the challenge of meshing different styles and temperaments, mastery of frustrations and conflicts, and the fun and comfort of doing and being together. But it takes a long time to build a sound relationship, and with siblings, there are special wrinkles involved that are explored in this book.

One is that the children feel themselves in competition not only for elbow room and possessions but for their parents' love and attention, a feeling that complicates the creation of a relationship on its own terms. Another is that siblings live together and cannot easily escape the intensity of their feelings for each other, both positive and negative: cooling-off periods, necessary in any relationship, are not easy to come by.

A third wrinkle, and the most complex, is that parents tend to invest their children with their own histories. A vigorous, strong-minded young daughter may evoke in a father reverberations of his early struggles with a bossy older sister. A mother may feel discomfort at her son's sensitivity and shyness because it reminds her of her own continuing efforts to be assertive. Children may even be reminders of our own parents, the grandparent generation, not only because of physical resemblance but because of our own unfinished growing up. Which of us has not carried into our adult lives feelings about our parents' authority over us as children, that then shaped how we attempted to control our own offspring, as if they were representatives of the past?

The hazards of laying the past on present children lie in our subsequent tendency to treat them as if they were indeed that long-ago sister, or self, or parent, instead of their unique selves. When that happens, the dynamic daughter may be prevented from pursuing her own independent path as a way of compensating for our personal insecurities. Or children may be dominated or coddled according to their fantasized connection to our earlier relationships with our own parents.

On the other hand, becoming part of the human family does involve, to some extent, inheriting not only bone structure and eye color but parental myths, fantasies, and memories. My mother often told my sister and me stories about her early life with her siblings: her feeling, as a middle child among five, of being loved less than the others; the way her older sister told jokes to keep her laughing and then sneaked food off her plate; her affection for her stylish younger sister. I, in turn, have shared these with my own daughter. They become, through the retelling, a part of our family culture. We all have a strong human need to make generational connections; there are strengths as well as hazards for children in feeling themselves linked to their parents' past lives. The point is that children in a family must work out what they mean to each other, not only in relation to their daily interaction but in the context of their family history, for better or for worse. In each family the intense angers, jealousies, resentments, anxieties, and vengeances that normally surround a growing sibling relationship (and this book emphasizes the normalcy of such feelings) have different meanings largely because of different histories.

In one family, arguments and name calling are seen as unacceptable rudeness; in another, they are evidence of self-confident assertiveness; in still another they spell affection. Competition is admired by some parents and forbidden by others. What is viewed as polite by one will seem obsequious to another. These differences stem from different past experiences, both satisfying and painful, in coping with human challenges. As they learn about each other, brothers and sisters are also learning their parents' and ancestors' definitions, values, styles, and preferences. They are learning what a family means, as the real-life anecdotes in this volume richly illustrate.

In some ways, the most important message of this book is that intense interactions between brothers and sisters—the love and hate, alliance and competition, protectiveness and rejection—are a normal fact of life. With the entry of a second child into a family, a drama begins—and continues with each new addition. Older children may demand attention by whining, getting into trouble, or developing skills and capacities so as to evoke praise and admiration. They may directly attack the baby or show anger by shouting or fighting with other children. They may hug the baby so hard it hurts. They may hide their real feelings and develop physical symptoms instead, like rashes or nail-biting. They may want to spend all their time at cribside, watching every infant move with hawkish attention. They may take up old ways again, like bed-wetting or thumb-sucking. They will likely also enjoy the baby's charms, being protective (sometimes overly so) and loving and proud. And they will surely take satisfaction in the privileges of now being "the big one."

The baby in turn, and any additional babies, will react to the older siblings with their own mélange of feelings and behaviors: admiration for big-sister/brother accomplishments, envy of special privileges, frustration at never being able to "catch up," resentment at being bossed, security in the knowledge that a reliable defender is on hand. Both sets of responses show caring and involvement, providing the basis for genuine intimacy and sharing. But neither is simple or smooth.

These matters are difficult to live with, primarily because of the personal reverberations they evoke. Indeed, an important aspect of parenting is the reliving of one's own childhood: Each developmental stage our children go through evokes its counterpart in our own lives. And therein lies the richness of parenting, the opportunity it provides for fresh understanding of our own past. So as we parent our children, in a sense we can reparent ourselves. The wisdom of this book lies in its implicit acknowledgment of that process.

—Dorothy W. Gross, Ed.D.

1

Sibling Rivalry: A Fact of Life

When Jack and I got married, we wanted to have lots of babies and raise a big family. But now all the kids do is squabble and fight. It's driving us right up the wall.

At times it may be hard for you to accept, but the fact is that sibling rivalry is, to a large degree, perfectly normal and natural. The battle between brothers and sisters (in all their various combinations) is one of the most basic and universal of family relationships, and stories of such rivalries go all the way back to the Bible and beyond.

In the pages that follow we'll talk about these conflicts in detail and will offer suggestions to help you live with them—and cope with them—more comfortably. Of course, there aren't any magic formulas or instant cures guaranteed to turn your own family group into a model of bliss and perfection. But these practical ideas may help you put sibling squabbles in perspective and show you how to deal with them constructively. Keep in mind that, in general, rivalry and competition between your children is a natural, healthy part of the growing process. There will be some bumps along the way, but the way *can* be made a lot less rocky for both parents and children—and as they continue to grow, your children will need your continuing help, guidance, and love.

The eminent pediatrician Dr. T. Berry Brazelton says that "sibling rivalry is not an evil born of parental failure. It is a fact of life." Like many facts of life, it is one that seems less threatening and makes us less anxious once we've examined, grasped, and then coped with the situation.

REAL VERSUS IDEAL

Once upon a time there was a family named Perfect. It consisted of Mother Perfect, Father Perfect, Sister Perfect, and Baby Brother Perfect. The Perfects loved one another like crazy. They never fought or argued. Mother and Father Perfect adored their children and never scolded or punished them. Sister Perfect adored Baby Brother Perfect, and he, tiny though he was, thought Sister Perfect was a living doll. So parents and children lived together, happily and perfectly, ever after . . .

Fairy tales are fun, of course, but everyone knows they're somewhat too good to be true. *Real* and *perfect* are two different things, and in every ideal situation reality has a sneaky way of creeping in. Real life, with its joys and satisfactions, also has its ups and downs, disappointments and frustrations—and conflicts inside the family circle. Many adults squabble, and so do most children. Why? Because being human means having human needs and feelings, and sometimes these needs and feelings aren't always cozy or convenient. This is especially so in the complex, half-formed, puzzling world of the very young.

What makes kids tick? How can you as a parent best understand your children's needs and motives—especially in the area of sibling rivalry? And will this understanding help you in dealing with family conflicts? Yes, of course—but understanding by itself won't eliminate conflicts. Nothing can specifically do that—nor should it. A good deal of competition between siblings is, in fact, essential to their development. So the real challenge for a parent is not to try to eliminate rivalry, but to keep it within healthy and constructive bounds.

Some parents tend to build up unreal, idealized expectations of how their children will relate to each other. In doing this, parents may relive their own sibling histories; they may think, for example, "I never got along with my brothers/sisters, but with my kids, it's going to be different." Such expectations, rooted in adults' perceptions of their own childhoods, are human—but they can be a trap. Each new generation must, and can, work out its own path to its own physical and emotional goals.

The world of our children is certainly different in many ways from the world of our own childhood, and they, like us, must make their own developmental journeys. To realize this is the first step in understanding, but insight and knowledge can do much more. They can give us new tools to work with, fresh ideas to help us minimize some of the trouble spots—also to be more tolerant of others. In short, insight can help you as a parent to be objective and to keep your children's squabbles in proper focus.

Let's remember that, up to a point, friction between siblings is indeed normal and healthy. As our kids' bodies slowly, steadily grow, their minds and personalities grow as well. They start to develop a sense of their own place in the scheme of things—a relationship to themselves, to their families, to the big world around them. This type of growth isn't as visible or apparent as physical growth, but we know it's there. We know that, like an invisible seed planted deep inside, the child's sense of identity (along with bodily changes) slowly forms and develops. And his or her need to test and strive, to compare and compete, is part of this process.

IDENTITY IS THE KEY

Put simply, competition among young siblings is their way of groping toward "selfhood"—the precious sense of individuality that we all need. This quest, rooted in *feelings,* is as important to children as it is to adults.

Think about it. Do you ever feel jealous or envious? Do

you sometimes like to compare yourself with others and "show off" a bit? Do you get upset when your feelings are hurt? Or when you think your rights are being ignored? Have you ever had a whopper of a fight with someone you love deeply? Well, it isn't abnormal. In moderation, those feelings are part of every person's deep inner urge for self-esteem and self-worth. Part of a natural desire for personal identity and for, as one psychiatrist puts it, a sense of "belonging to oneself."

Vegetables don't have emotions or identity needs. People do—and children are people. Among the very young these deep drives are even more powerful than ours, because kids don't have our built-in ego safeguards or the protective rules of social behavior that we acquire as we grow up.

Does this mean children have *no* standards of behavior? Not at all—but in general they're somewhat different. One team of researchers, Drs. Bossard and Boll, points out, "Adults judge child behavior by adult standards; children judge it by child standards." These "kid codes" (concepts of fairness, rights of ownership, and so on) are basic, simple, and cruder than our own. But they're just as strong and just as valid.

As a parent, your job—not always easy—is to recognize these drives as essential, and to help as much as possible to channel them successfully.

CHAPTER
2

The Roots of Rivalry

I hate Monica! She's a pest! She always breaks my toys. She butts in when I'm playing with my friends. I don't care if she's my little sister—I hate her!

A rival, according to the dictionary, is "a person who is competing for the same object or goal as another, or who tries to equal or outdo another; a competitor."

Among siblings (brothers and sisters in the same family unit), rivalry is all too familiar. And sometimes very hard to live with! Where does it come from, anyway? What makes siblings fight and squabble the way they do? Many of the answers, which aren't really mysterious, can be found woven through your child's immediate world—the basic family unit.

FAMILY MATTERS

Sibling relationships and family relationships go together. The two are firmly bonded, so it would be almost impossible to understand sibling rivalry without first taking a look at the family itself.

Some experts refer to the makeup of the family as a "constellation"—and like constellations in the night sky, families do have distinct patterns and groupings. But there's one major difference: Where our star groups are relatively fixed and unchanging, the constellation of the family is constantly shifting and developing. More important, the separate parts of this constellation act and interact with each other; every member of your own family circle has an effect on every other member (for better or worse!) and the arrival of each new baby changes and alters the pattern. This applies not just to parents but to children as well, because families are like living organisms, always growing and adapting to new conditions.

When Socrates, the great Greek philosopher, was an old man, he began to study music and dancing. It never occurred to him that he was "too old" for this—learning was simply a built-in part of his life process. So with all of us this very human process, conscious or not, rarely stops. Growth isn't the private property of young people. Nor is it limited to physical matters. As adults we also continue to grow, and in so doing influence the children whom we care for and nurture. In our day-to-day growth and interaction, we develop into integrated people capable of living in society. In other words, each family is a small facsimile of society as a whole—a kind of training ground where young siblings learn how to be successful adults.

The family constellation—this mini-society—has many dimensions. On one hand, it serves as a support system; on the other, it acts as a pressure cooker. The very same family that gives its members warmth, security, and love can also generate tension, discord, and upsets. But by and large this is to be expected. Some experts claim that a family that's always sublimely peaceful would be an unnatural, even an unwholesome one. Because when human beings live closely together, there's bound to be friction and disagreement. Our viewpoints often vary, as do our needs and desires, and within the family these constantly bump up against the needs and wishes of other members.

LIFTING THE LID

There's another reason for such conflicts. The family unit serves adults and children as both a haven and a safety valve. It's one place where our deep, honest feelings can be expressed—where we can lift the lid and really let off steam. In the outside world we usually have to be on our good behavior. Even in today's open and permissive society, there are codes we're expected to follow. This applies to adults in offices, shops, and factories as well as to kids in classrooms and on their playing fields. But in the privacy and safety of home, the codes of behavior can be altered; here at last is a refuge where we can "let it all hang out" without fear of serious rejection. Add to this the fact that, for children, home is their basic testing ground, and we see ample reason for the kinds of battles that may erupt.

Personalities within families will certainly clash, often with a kind of heightened intensity. This shouldn't come as a surprise when we realize that as family members, we depend upon and love each other much more intensely than we do outsiders, and we're prone to express our deeper feelings more openly within this circle.

Are your own kids, away from home, models of polite, sensible conduct? Do you ever get compliments on how considerate and well behaved they are? And when those same kids get back on home ground, does the chaos start all over again? If we accept and understand the concept of "family as safety valve," the pattern (difficult or not) will at least make some sense.

Does this mean that families are supposed to function without rules and regulations? No, of course not; we do need fair codes of conduct that will be respected and enforced. Living as a family unit is an art, and socializing our children means teaching them to be considerate of others, to shun violence, to avoid emotional extremes and excesses. Rules are also valuable because they give children a necessary sense of security. We know that kids have powerful inner drives that they can't always handle. In a way, growing up is like having a tiger by the tail, and without some sense of limits and controls the world, to a child, can seem very frightening.

Steven M., now an adult, recalls being brought up in a family guided by what was then the faddish notion of total permissiveness. In his home he was reared with an almost complete absence of social rules or guidelines—the watchword was "anything goes." But instead of giving young Steven a comfortable sense of freedom, this made him anxious and had a decidedly negative effect: "My folks never chastised me or stopped me or put any limits on my behavior. So I grew up thinking they really didn't care. Their aim was well intentioned, but the message that came through was that they were indifferent to me."

At the other end of the spectrum, and just as harmful, is the unbending discipline that turns a home into a military camp, with endless, complex rules and regulations. So it's reasonable to say that the best path lies somewhere between total hands-off child rearing and the harsh inflexibility of earlier times. The rigid, stifling codes of Victorian life, when children were very strictly monitored and were seen and not heard have gone the way of gaslight and high-button shoes. In contrast, today's families are much more relaxed and free. We're more successful now at communicating, at showing the kind of openness and tolerance that are so vital to our own and our children's well-being.

Keep in mind that if life seemed simpler and smoother in "the good old days," this was true only on the surface. In those days, many emotional conflicts were quietly swept under the rug—hardly a healthy solution. Fortunately, modern parents have more flexibility, are much better equipped to face sibling and other problems, and can deal with them more honestly. Some of these family flashpoints—as we'll see—can be corrected or eliminated simply by using common sense; others, of course, are more complex, calling for patience and understanding. And in some difficult cases, professional help may be needed.

It's good to remember, too, that, with growing children, not all problems are settled permanently. The same difficulties may arise next year or the year after, in new and different forms. Progress is certainly possible; but it's slow and uneven, and the conflicts themselves will change as the children grow.

SHIFTING PATTERNS

Life is a process of constant change and growth—and families reflect this in many ways.

Your first baby, for instance, was born into a family that consisted of two parents (or possibly only one parent). So we have a small constellation in which a great deal of adult concern and love can be focused on a single infant. In time a second baby is born. This infant, unlike the first, now enters a group consisting of two parents plus an older sibling. The third child joins a unit of *four* people, and so on. While this may seem a trivial point, it's important in helping to understand your siblings' personality patterns.

A child's "order of birth" is arbitrary—it's an event over which none of us has any control—but there are various advantages and disadvantages connected with this order. The first child, for example, will enjoy (at least for a while) a unique status. He or she is the hub of parental attention and concern—a tiny monarch seated on a throne, without peer or challenger. Parents also tend to have very high expectations and standards for their first beloved offspring.

In some ways the second child can never usurp the position of this other sibling. No matter how hard he or she tries, the first will always be older, bigger, usually more advanced. On the other hand, parents are often calmer and more relaxed with baby number two. They've learned from earlier mistakes and experiences, so a second child may be subjected to less underlying tension and anxiety. Parents may also make fewer demands on this second offspring than they did on the first.

Child number three is sometimes more "spoiled," more indulged and pampered, especially if the older siblings have grown to school age. In addition, child number three now has two siblings on whom to model his or her conduct. The older children often act as the new family member's mentors and teachers.

There are other variations with the fourth and fifth child, with twins, and so on. We'll look closely at these advantages and disadvantages of birth order in the next chapter; suffice it to mention here that there will be emerging differences as your family grows. The accident of being born first, last, or in-between does play a part in each child's experiences and in the patterns of a family constellation. Have you ever caught yourself saying, "Your sister never acted like this," or "Why can't you behave politely, like your little brother?" If so, it helps to realize that some behavior can be due, in part, to basic differences in the order of birth.

THE AGE GAP

Sibling rivalry depends not only on family makeup and birth order, but also on the age span between children.

Experts generally agree that jealousy and rivalry are more intense when the age gap between siblings is from one and a half to three years. Here the gap is narrow, and patterns of development are fairly similar, which leads to greater friction. An age span of four or five years reduces competition between siblings, since they share fewer immediate needs and activities. Similarly, a gap of six years or more means less and less rivalry. A six-year-old, busy with school and other widening interests, has a reasonably good sense of identity—of his or her secure place in the scheme of things—and a new baby is no longer seen as a serious challenge to this position.

SEX SIMILARITIES

Surveys indicate, too, that, in many cases, there's more jealousy between same-sex siblings than between those of opposite sex. Here again two children of the same sex, close in age, will have a lot of common needs and interests, and this generates more quarrels and conflict.

One mother with two girls, age three and five, says,

> Jill and Betsy are always at each other. They both want each other's toys, each other's clothes, everything. They even fight over who should be "mother" when they play house. Yesterday I had to take Betsy, my youngest, to the doctor—and Jill insisted on coming, too. Imagine asking to go to the doctor! Of course she didn't want any part of him, but she hated the idea that for a little while Betsy would have me all to herself.

All this is manageable—and can be lived with. The important thing is to ensure that each family member has a generous share of love, attention, and consideration. The challenge is to treat each of your children as an individual. When a parent sits down and works out a problem with a child, that child is helped to feel his or her individuality and to develop a personal sense of pride and worthiness. This feeling, reinforced on a day-to-day basis, helps every child—whether the first, second, or tenth—to grasp that he or she really does belong, not only to home and family but eventually to the wider world.

MEASURING AND MIRRORING

Perhaps there's a place on your wall somewhere, or in your child's room, where you've kept a record of how he or she is growing, month by month and year by year. The age-old ritual is an enjoyable one. Your child stands against the wall, out come pencil and ruler, and a new mark is made, to be compared proudly with the mark made previously. Other skills and milestones are also noted: "Look, Mommy, I tied my own shoes!" or "I went to the toilet all by myself!" or "Daddy, watch how I ride my bike!" and so on. And later, when school begins, youngsters bring home their grades and report cards, which keep track of their progress.

These things obviously help us and our children to measure all the exciting changes taking place. Yet, at the same time, a natural *inner* growth is going on—the development of ego, identity, a sense of status and self-worth. These are much harder to measure and evaluate, but kids have their own methods. And that's where siblings often come in. Instinctively, children learn to judge themselves not only by what parents say, but by measuring their skills and competencies against those of their peers. And the handiest, most convenient peers for this purpose are brothers and sisters in the immediate family, especially when age levels are close.

So in a sense, siblings use each other as mirrors in which to see who they are and who they *can* be. Younger siblings pattern themselves on older ones and try to emulate their achievements. Older siblings compare themselves with younger ones to see how far they've come and to gain a sense of progress and accomplishment. At times they may also act as a younger sibling's teacher and mentor, which adds to the older child's self-esteem.

ACTIONS AND INTERACTIONS

Your family, every family, is a marvelous living network—parents interacting with parents, children interacting with parents, children interacting with children—and this vital process leads to self-knowledge. In short, children in the family learn things about themselves by "bouncing off" one another. But this, we know, isn't smooth or simple.

Sibling relationships can and do involve warmth, love, and sharing; but often the interaction leads to friction and fights, challenges and accusations, anger and jealousy, resentment and hurt feelings. And all this is heightened by the fact that kids (especially the younger ones) aren't very subtle. Their language is blunt. Their behavior is instinctive. Their feelings are direct and primitive. Kids don't say, "I find your attitude upsetting to me," or "I don't approve of the way you're behaving." They say "I hate you!"—and that's that.

In the private circle of the family, these strong emotions pour out openly. As we've already seen, the family acts as a kind of safety valve, a place where words and feelings can have fairly free play without being covered up. Of course we have rules and regulations, but in this safe haven children are better able to measure and test themselves freely. So when the going gets rough, remind yourself that no child can conveniently slip on a "handy identity" the way one might put on a sweater or dress or pair of jeans. For each child a sense of self comes from deep inside, growing as the child grows. As you know from your own childhood, it's a slow, painful struggle, and there are no easy paths or shortcuts.

But all this measuring and mirroring is only one part of the sibling picture. Other strong drives are also at work, as children try to establish a fragile footing in an overwhelming world.

JOCKEYING FOR POWER

"She got the biggest piece of cake!"
"If he can stay up to watch TV, so can I!"
"Mom, Julie didn't brush her teeth!"
"It isn't fair—he never has to help in the kitchen!"
"If you touch my things again, I'll smack you!"

Yes, the squabbling does go on and on, and it's usually about small, unimportant things. As a parent you know about the arguments and endless hassles "over nothing," and perhaps you've asked yourself why kids make so much fuss over trivial matters. Is an extra cookie or fifteen minutes more of "stay-up time" all that important to them?

The answer is yes—but not necessarily for the reasons

you'd expect. Because most of the daily friction between kids involves more than what shows on the surface. Dr. Alfred Adler, the famed psychologist and former student of Sigmund Freud, was one of the first, years ago, to explore this age-old question of sibling conflict. Today some experts play down his findings, but in general they're of great value in helping us understand our children.

According to Dr. Adler, a lot of "kid squabbling" is really based on a subconscious striving for power. Adler writes, "One must remember that every child occupies an inferior position in life; were it not for a certain quantum of social feeling on the part of his family he (or she) would be incapable of independent existence." The "certain quantum of social feeling" he mentions is the free outpouring of parental care and acceptance, and without this nurturing—without some nurturing—a young child would find it impossible to survive. Think of how weak and helpless, how totally dependent, a newborn infant is! Think of how its very life depends on one or more adults who will feed it, change it, keep it warm and safe. We humans do start out as very fragile beings; our innate sense of helplessness (which goes back to birth) is a real fact of life. It is experienced by children everywhere and strongly influences later attitudes and actions.

Every child starts out with these natural feelings of inadequacy, and in trying to handle these feelings—and master them—the child seeks power. Or what passes for power in a child's small world. Psychologists point out that kids don't necessarily strive for power as such, but for a semblance of it. Anyone who reads the daily newspapers knows that *real* power is a dangerous, tricky thing, but young children are quite content with its symbols. So winning a game of Candyland or winding up with a fair share of the cake or getting the front seat in the car can mean more to kids than we realize. These tiny triumphs give the child a satisfying sense of control. It's as if he or she can say, "See, I'm not so helpless after all!" No wonder, then, that brothers and sisters bicker and wrangle over seemingly trivial things. No wonder they struggle so stubbornly to "come out ahead."

CINDERELLA WAS A SIBLING, TOO

Other experts have studied this subject, among them the educators B. G. Rosenberg and Brian Sutton-Smith, and in a recent survey they noted that "the theme of sibling conflict as a struggle for power recurs throughout literary history."

We're all familiar with the Bible stories of Cain and Abel, Jacob and Esau, and the tale of Joseph, who was victimized by his older brothers. A pattern of sibling conflict turns up in many of our folk and fairy tales. In the fairy tales of the brothers Grimm, for example, sibling struggles often take place—and are usually won by the youngest child, who succeeds in outwitting adults as well as older brothers and sisters. We also know the classic success story of Cinderella, who triumphs in the end over her cruel and powerful stepsisters. Given the young child's drive to overcome deep feelings of inadequacy, it's easy enough to understand why this particular story is so popular. We like to identify with literary heroes and heroines—and what child, regardless of age or sex, can fail to cheer for poor Cinderella and relish her final victory? Kids respond to folk and fairy tales for many reasons and on many levels, but it's clear that one reason these stories are cherished is because the youngest and weakest players often come out on top—they win the power battle, and are thus able to live "happily ever after."

Of course we have to be careful not to oversimplify, but this power battle does seem to be a part of sibling interaction. As each child in the family works to gain status and self-esteem, he or she may look upon brothers and sisters as somehow a threat to that goal. And this in turn promotes competition, jealousy, and resentment, which at times explode into anger.

COMPETING FOR PARENTAL LOVE

We can now see that sibling rivalry stems from mirroring and from a child's natural drive for power. But there's another, even stronger, force at work.

A great deal of competition between kids—most of it, at certain ages—is simply competition for parental love and approval. This may be disguised and covered up, but it remains the underlying motive. To a child, a parent's love is vital and all-important because it spells safety, security, and support. And since mother and father hold the real power within the family, their love is a kind of unwritten *guarantee of protection*.

This is something children learn from the beginning. Watch a baby while it's being held by somebody strange and unfamiliar. Most likely the baby will be anxious and uncomfortable. But notice how the infant's face lights up with pleasure and relief when a parent or other familiar adult comes into the room. Instinctively, our anxious baby connects the face with its own sense of security, and its fears fade away.

All humans, we know, have a primal urge to give and receive love. And among children the deepest need, the greatest hunger, is to receive love from the adult or adults on whom they depend for their very existence. Because of this dependence, young siblings sometimes fear that love given by parents to others will mean love withheld from themselves. In a later chapter we'll look at this view of love in some detail, but for now let's simply acknowledge the vital importance of these loving and nurturing feelings—to us and to our children.

LEARNING TO LIVE TOGETHER

It's also good to keep in mind that sibling conflicts, though real, aren't all that terribly serious. This kind of rivalry *is* natural, after all, and has many positive aspects. As children get older, they themselves become aware of this and are able to look at their own behavior more objectively. One teen-age girl had a bad squabble with her younger brother. Later, realizing she'd been unfair and childish, she made amends to him. Then she said to her mother, "I'm sorry I yelled at Timmy, Mom. I guess I just had a bad case of the 'sibbles.'"

Child psychologist Leah Levinger doesn't even like the term *sibling rivalry* and prefers to talk about *sibling affiliation.* Dr. Levinger wrote recently, "The very words 'sibling rivalry' have a cold, clinical note, which makes it seem more alarming and difficult to handle than 'brothers and sisters squabble, make up, love each other, squabble again.'"

In her sensitive phrasing we can almost feel the process of growth and testing taking place. Sibling conflict is indeed a complex, inevitable, and valuable part of a child's development. This conflict, irritating at times and (to parents) even irrational, does help youngsters to test and clarify their emotions, and to measure their progress against other "strugglers" like themselves.

All this is deftly summed up by Dr. T. Berry Brazelton, who points out that sibling rivalry "can be a major spur in children's learning to live together, learning how to share, how to win victories and suffer defeats, how to love and how to cope with their own unloving feelings." Dr. Brazelton further points out that children need to learn these lessons in childhood, and that failure to do so may make it far more difficult, and emotionally costly, to learn them later as adults.

CHAPTER
3

Places on the Ladder: Birth Order

Looking back on it, I think our first child had a tougher time because Marge and I were so inexperienced. By the time the second baby came, we were old hands. More relaxed, not so uptight. There's no doubt we fussed a lot over our first one, and we expected more of her—but we also made more mistakes.

What do Albert Einstein, William Shakespeare, Eleanor Roosevelt, Martin Luther King, Margaret Mead, Ludwig van Beethoven, Sigmund Freud, Marian Anderson, and Harry S Truman have in common? Aside from the fact that they became famous, they were all firstborn children with younger siblings.

Certainly not every firstborn is a high achiever, nor is the first particularly the "best" rung on the birth ladder. And not all great men and women are firstborn children. Mohandas K. Gandhi, Napoleon, Leo Tolstoy, Marie Curie, John F. Kennedy, and Susan B. Anthony, equally famous, all had older siblings. But studies carried out over many years do indicate certain general patterns and personality traits that relate to the birth order of a child. We can't, in fact, fully grasp the nature of sibling behavior without knowing a little something about the unique role played by this accidental order of a sibling's birth.

18

TRAITS AND PATTERNS

Until fairly recently, it was felt that children were molded and influenced chiefly by parental actions and attitudes, but studies now show that a lot of personality conditioning is based on the influence of their siblings as well. When we deal with people and personalities, of course, we can't generalize too much; there are no hard-and-fast rules, and each person is different. But certain patterns do seem to recur with predictability.

Why does one child seem more sure of himself/herself than another? Why is this child shy, that child a bully, another one a schemer? Why do some kids lack self-confidence? Why are some more aggressive than their siblings? More fearful? When children show negative traits or minor shortcomings, parents often ask themselves, "What did we do wrong?" But we know now that the answers to such matters may have to do, to an extent, with the birth order of each child in the family constellation. This is obviously a matter of chance; where each child winds up in the hierarchy is beyond anyone's control. But each spot on the family ladder has certain broad advantages and disadvantages. So, to understand personality fully, we do have to consider the specific place of each child in the constellation.

It begins with the classic two-sibling family, but of course when a third baby is born, the youngest becomes a middle sibling, changing the relationships. We also have families with four, five, six, or more youngsters, families with twins, and others with children from earlier marriages. All these form varying patterns, but the birth position of each individual child plays a role throughout. One researcher, Dr. Walter Toman, claims that order of birth marks a child's total personality, adult social behavior, even the nature of his or her marriage.

Whether such claims are fully supportable, it's a fact that birth order makes a difference in growth experience. But the place in which a child is born—first, last, in between—isn't necessarily "good" or "bad"; there are benefits and draw-backs to each. Remember, too, that we can only generalize, since every child is different, family circumstances vary greatly, and life patterns are never identical.

It sometimes comes as a surprise to parents to realize that *no two children are ever born into the exact same family.* Keeping this in mind, let's take a brief look at the specific rungs on the sibling ladder.

THE FIRSTBORN CHILD

Your firstborn, psychologists tell us, begins life with power, and with a "special access" to parental figures. Baby number one is certainly the family's first star; for a while at least, the oldest child is the only child, an infant of privilege, center of all attention.

Since the firstborn enjoys a central position, in which mother and father *do not have to be shared with others,* this can leave a positive, indelible stamp on the child's self-confidence and self-esteem. For the first years of life, your firstborn is involved with child-*parent* relationships rather than child-*child* relationships. As a result, according to researcher Irving Harris, the firstborn's position "gives him a certain self-righteousness." Harris and others maintain that because this child's earliest memories have to do exclusively with adults, he or she will be more receptive to authority, more consistent, and morally more rigid. Firstborns tend to be more sure of themselves. Also, unlike younger siblings, they're inclined to fight stubbornly rather than make compromises. Perhaps this explains why a large proportion of firstborns become successful executives, politicians, and military leaders.

But despite its privileges, the position of number one has its drawbacks, too. Mother and father are still inexperienced as parents, so they're more likely to make mistakes. They'll also be more anxious and uptight about their duties, and this uncertainty may be transmitted to the infant.

Mary T., an executive now in her forties, recalls her earliest years:

As a child I was rather frail; and since I was the first, my parents were constantly hovering over me, worrying about my health. There were a lot of things I wasn't allowed to eat. I could never climb trees or play rough games with the other kids. My mother seemed to be forever taking my temperature; feeling my forehead to see if I had a fever. I was seven when my baby brother came along. Then they relaxed a little. But they were always more easygoing with Frank and overprotective of me. I grew up a rather timid person; not very sure of myself. To this day I'm anxious about testing my own limits and taking risks, which is possibly holding me back some in my career.

Parents are also, in many ways, stricter with the first child than with later ones. Because he or she is older, the firstborn is often expected to serve as a model to the others, to be more dependable, responsible, and mature. Firstborns are familiar with admonitions like, "You're older, and you should know better." Or, "Since you're the oldest, you're supposed to set a good example." Such comments put unfair pressure on an older child and can stir up resentment and anxiety. They're really a form of comparison between siblings and, as such, should be avoided.

Pressured or not, the oldest child does sense these expectations; in part, the high achievement levels of firstborns may be due to adult attitudes that are subtly built into a growing child's thinking. We know that parents can transfer private fantasies to their children, especially to their firstborn. Whatever a frustrated adult's ambitions may have been, these can be displaced onto the next generation: "He/she will accomplish everything I failed to accomplish." Subconscious thinking of this type obviously plays a part in a young child's development.

Mark L., a carpenter and father of three, talks of his own father's expectations.

My dad was a working man; struggled most of his life, never got anywhere. I was the only boy, and he pinned all his hopes on me. Wanted me to get a good education, which I did, and then go into a fancy profession. You know, law or science or banking. Well, all I *really* wanted to do was work with my hands—to be a good carpenter and cabinetmaker. We fought about it, but I stuck to my guns. I love what I'm doing; if I say so myself, I'm pretty good at it. But I don't think the old man ever forgave me or really understood. Anyway, Sally and I try not to pressure our own kids about their careers. Advice and support, yes—the rest is up to them.

We all try to live up to expectations, and firstborns are surely no exception. So as a parent, ask yourself, "Are my demands on him (or her) fair and reasonable? Are they within the child's scope and abilities? Am I trying to gain success vicariously through our youngster?" Care and sensitivity are needed here so as not to turn a parent's hopes into a sibling's burdens.

Finally, the arrival of a second baby and the "dethroning" of the first can be traumatic for an older child and calls for special psychological adjustments that the second or third child won't have to make. In addition, your firstborn, in spite of his or her apparent self-sufficiency, may need shielding from the immature behavior of the little ones. The oldest sib's needs and rights are every bit as important as those of the younger infant in the family. Doing homework, practicing the guitar, working on a hobby—whatever the child's activity, he or she is entitled to a full share of time and privacy without interference from younger siblings. And of course your firstborn, no matter *how* capable and mature, will go on needing your guidance and involvement through the years.

THE SECOND CHILD

In families with two children, there are four possible combinations:
  · Older sister with younger brother
  · Older sister with younger sister

· Older brother with younger brother
· Older brother with younger sister

As we've noted, competition and rivalry between siblings is usually most intense when the kids are closer in age—where the span between them is three years or less. It also seems more pronounced when siblings are of the same sex. Two young brothers or young sisters living close together in a family unit will obviously have many parallel needs and interests; and because of this similarity and overlapping there's fertile ground for rivalry. The friction can be likened to a fierce, daily tug-of-war in which both parties are almost evenly matched—which leads to much more stress and strain than when the contestants are matched less closely.

In a two-sibling family, the older one almost always holds an edge, but the younger child can compensate by psychological means. Lacking the age advantage, fated to trail behind the older sibling, child number two may become adept at manipulating, at teasing, at egging on the older one. As one young man recalls a bit sheepishly, "When I was little, I'd try to push my big sister into doing something wrong. Then I'd have the secret pleasure of seeing her punished."

Most second siblings profit from their parents' earlier mistakes, since father and mother have learned the hard way, by trial and error. The younger sib feels pressure, of course, because the firstborn stays a few crucial jumps ahead. At the same time, living with this older role model can help a youngster advance much more rapidly. Thus second children often learn to play games or ride bikes or dress themselves at an earlier point. The older sib serves as a spur and an example; watch any child diligently imitating big brother or big sister, and you'll notice the marvelously accelerated learning that takes place.

Growing up under less restraint, with more relaxed parents, child number two also tends to be somewhat more free, more adventurous, less rigid about "the rules." In many ways, there are fewer demands on this sibling, since parental concern is now divided between two children instead of being focused on one.

THE MIDDLE CHILD

"I was in the middle, so I never got any of the advantages."
"The child in the middle is usually neglected."
"Being in the middle, I lost out to the older one *and* the baby."

Comments like these, though familiar, aren't necessarily accurate. As a family expands, subtle shifts take place that resemble the childhood game of musical chairs. The firstborn child will always remain the firstborn, but other roles change as each child moves up the ladder.

In general, the middle child does have a reputation for being somewhat overlooked. After all, his or her arrival wasn't as wonderfully exciting as the arrival of the firstborn. Nor is a middle child generally as cherished or doted upon as the youngest, the baby of the family. But the place of the middle child or children has benefits and carries with it specific opportunities. Let's consider some of these.

Before baby number three arrived, middle child was the youngest family member. In a way the firstborn was a "guinea pig," but with the second, mother and father have usually learned a lot about what and what not to do; so this child is spared a good bit of nervous fuss and anxiety. With the arrival of baby number three, parental attention shifts, freeing the middle child, to a degree, from some restrictions. Because of the general easing of limits and attitudes, your in-between child may become adventuresome and daring, also less of a conformist than the others. Neither burdened by responsibilities like the oldest, nor pampered like the youngest, the middle child is more able to take chances and to accept challenges. The middle one also has the advantage of an older sibling who can serve as a role model. Conversely, there's now a younger child on hand, whom he or she can help to teach and nurture.

In an effort to win status, middles are also spurred on to develop their personal skills and talents, learning to excel at sports or becoming adept in certain of the arts and so on. Once they take on this challenge, middle children often wind up outperforming older sibs in those activities that are not dependent upon age and size.

Balancing all this there are, of course, a few drawbacks. The middle child is destined to live always in the firstborn's shadow. Ahead of him or her there stands the older sibling, enjoying all the privileges of that position. Invariably, the older will be first to get the two-wheeler, first to have new (and more grown-up) clothes, first to stay up late, first to read and write and go to school.

This gap can never be fully closed, but as we've seen, middle sibs develop their own ways of coping with it. Some may become manipulators, cajoling older brothers and sisters and gaining their goals in subtle, roundabout ways.

On the other side of the middle child stands the youngest, usually a recipient of special attention, perhaps the most cherished and protected. Just as the middle child can never reach the status of the older, so, too, he or she may never regain the love and attention that seem to be lavished on the younger. This may result in a lack of self-esteem for the middle sib, and here again parents have a key responsibility. Their role can and must be to keep the middle child from feeling unfairly put upon or neglected. This doesn't take great amounts of time and effort, but it does take a little extra care, thought, and sensitivity. The middle child will certainly feel less "disadvantaged" if he or she is treated lovingly, as a unique and valued individual.

Depending on age and sex differences, the middle child may form a special bond with one or the other of the siblings. If the firstborn is a good bit older, the two younger sibs are apt to gravitate toward one another. If the ages between first and second are close, these two will probably form a special relationship. Where there are four siblings, the two in the middle will often be closer—both in friendship and in rivalry.

Anne W., a dietician in San Francisco, remembers her own close relationship with a younger sister:

> I was in the middle. Beth was two years younger than I was. Jeff, our brother, was six years older. As a kid and a teenager, he was a hotshot athlete—very good, really the center of the family. Jeff didn't pay any mind to us girls, hardly even noticed us. And as I say, he got most of the attention at home. Beth and I could have been rivals, I guess, but instead we formed a kind of coalition. Maybe we were early "women's lib," who knows? But we drew together as children, and we're still close. I think it started as a defense, but it worked well for us. Jeff was important to my parents, and we were important to each other.

The noted author of *Winnie the Pooh,* A. A. Milne, was the third son of a London schoolmaster. He formed a particularly close bond with his next older brother, Ken, and the two boys were inseparable. They fought a good deal, supported each other emotionally, even collaborated in composing light verse, which they published under a combined name. This relationship was, in many ways, a classic of sibling rivalry. Milne wrote later in his autobiography, "We never ceased to quarrel with each other—nor to feel the need for each other." Based on such accounts, it's reasonable to say that siblings gain strength not in spite of the squabbling but *because* of the squabbling, which somehow serves as a psychological cement to weld the young competitors together. So this ability to move in either direction—bonding with either an older sib or a younger one—does constitute another hidden advantage for those born in the middle.

Sex differences also play a special role with middle kids. If the middle child is the only girl, with brothers on each side, or the only boy, with sisters on each side, the self-esteem of the middle child will likely be higher. Being the only girl or only boy does give this child a sense of uniqueness, of being special in the family, and this adds greatly to the child's sense of personal worth. Which again supports the fact that all children hunger for a feeling of uniqueness—a hunger that can be filled when parents spend positive time with their middleborns, helping them to develop their own special abilities and talents.

THE YOUNGEST CHILD

A San Diego mother and nurse, now in her thirties, recalls,

I was the youngest in our family and had two brothers and a sister before me. The closest one, my sister, was four years older. So in many ways, I was the center of attention; I was babied and fussed over quite a bit, even by the older kids. Of course I enjoyed it, but I do think it held me back a little. It may have kept me from growing up, facing the challenges.

The youngest in the family, like all siblings, has to contend with both the plusses and the minuses of birth order. Generally, the baby of the group tends to be overindulged and overprotected, which may foster dependency and a lack of self-reliance. Balancing this, the youngest child has one or more siblings to serve as physical examples and to help him or her learn and grow. By tagging along with the older kids, trying constantly to do what they do, the youngest often makes faster progress and gains valuable early experience.

Youngest children also tend to be friendlier and more gregarious than first or middle sibs and are popular with other children. Used to working with and relating to a range of ages, they're comfortable with their peers outside the family and take readily and easily to group activities. So while they may not always have a strong self-image, they are rarely withdrawn or loner types.

The youngest also has the widest choice of sibling relationships. Here, as always, much depends on an individual family's composition and the age range between the siblings.

The firstborn in a family may be old enough to play a real and significant part in caring for the youngest. In large family groups, oldest and youngest often form a special kind of "parent-child" bond, unique and personal. Sibling rivalry usually arises between the youngest and the nearest sibling— the one closest in age. With only a few years separating these two, classic patterns of competition will develop—which can be helpful and of ultimate value to both.

Charlie T., a commercial fisherman in New England, was the youngest of six children. He recalls,

> There were three boys, then two girls, then me. When I was little, my older brothers were kind of remote. There was such an age gap between us, they seemed so big, almost godlike to me; but they were supportive. They babied me and enjoyed teaching me things as I got older. Still, there was never any question of rivalry with them; it was impossible. For that I had my sister Nina, who was only two years older than I was. When it came to testing myself, she was kind of my rival. The older boys were my models, but Nina was the one who I could *really* compete with or play games with, roughly as an equal. Sure, we scrapped all the time—but we were real close to each other. Still are.

Of course there are some drawbacks to being youngest. Studies show that although the youngest sib rarely feels neglected, there may be a marked sense of dependency and powerlessness. In part, this is because the youngest, at the bottom of the sibling ladder, is furthest removed from the focus of parental power and authority. Childhood years are spent surrounded by siblings who are bigger, older, more advanced. *Everyone*—so it seems to the youngest—can do things better than he or she can. And all this puts special pressure on the young one, who, in spite of pampering, may feel that catching up to the others is an insurmountable task.

The youngest sib, used to much attention, may also tend to be bossy. These little psychological games, coming naturally to the youngest sib, are seen by this child as one way to correct the sense of being powerless.

Sex differences play a part here, too. Researchers find that a boy baby with older sisters will have an easier time in relating to women later in life. Used to females in his family—and used to being indulged by them—he's generally relaxed and happy around women and can readily show warm, loving feelings. Similarly, a young girl with older brothers grows up feeling secure and well protected. In later years she usually gets along well with men; though her expectations, and possibly her demands, are high, she will value the males in her life and show affection for them easily.

THE ADULT YEARS

What happens to these positions on the birth ladder as the years pass and siblings get older? In many cases, competition between brothers and sisters goes on well into adulthood, but researchers also find that siblings may form deep loyalties with each other, which continue throughout their lives.

Dr. Margaret Mead, for example, referred in her autobiography to the warmth and closeness between herself and her younger sister, Elizabeth. In this context she wrote,

> Sisters, while they are growing up, tend to be very rivalrous, and as young mothers they are given to continuous rivalrous comparisons of their several children. But once the children grow older, sisters draw closer together and often, in old age, they become each other's chosen and most happy companions.

Among adult brothers, too, a form of "sibling solidarity" is often present. Boys who have been fiercely competitive as children can develop close affiliations as the years pass. The reason is obvious enough and gives a further clue to the earlier squabbling: As children grow into adults and develop stronger identities, there's less need for testing capacities with each other. In place of earlier all-out competition, they can allow other feelings to take over. One adult older brother noted recently,

> When we were kids, my younger brother and I fought constantly. Cats and dogs. We never got on too well with Father, who was rigid and very judgmental. But the rivalry with Ted was an outlet. And somehow it helped us form ties together. Ted and I count on each other—we have a kind of mutual support system going for us now.

This doesn't mean that competition between youthful siblings always disappears later on. In many cases it continues, though on different levels, just as personality and temperament continue. But it does point to the potentialities for strong bonding, when sibling rivals grow to adulthood.

THE PARENT'S ROLE

How do you, as a parent, keep your footing on this intriguing sibling ladder and deal with the complexities? Later we'll explore this in detail, but a few observations can be made here.

Birth order is the matrix in which young relationships are formed. Part of these relationships involves squabbling, competition, and striving among your children to gain "power." Since this rivalry is basically normal, transactions between siblings can best be left to *them* to work out by themselves, as far as possible.

The pattern of fighting . . . making up . . . fighting . . . making up . . . is a classic one, and contributes to needed development. What parents *can* do, however, is to be sure that an older child doesn't become a bully or use violence on a younger brother or sister. So it's best for parents to take a generally hands-off attitude, *except where the friction is violent or excessive.* It's also important for parents to keep an eye on an older sib lest he or she begin to victimize the younger, constantly taunting and criticizing. If these taunts become a fixed pattern, it may cause the young siblings to grow timid, lose confidence, and be afraid to take on new challenges. However, your younger child is not without subtle weapons. Unable to win on physical or mental grounds, he or she may resort to deviousness or chronic lying, which may set a precedent for later adult behavior. Of course this behavior should be discouraged.

In dealing with excesses, a parent doesn't have to be a psychologist or a secret agent; he or she simply has to be alert. Try to observe your children objectively, setting aside your own personal feelings. Listen to what they say. Apply a bit of common sense. With well-tuned antennae, sensitive parents can almost always spot signs of real trouble and can step in to ward it off.

Also, keep in mind that kids use words in a different way than we do as adults. Their expressions are crude and extreme simply because they aren't capable yet of the more subtle nuances of language. So, when an older child shouts, "I *hate* the baby!" or when a young one says of an older sib, "I wish he (or she) would die!" they're expressing momentary anger with very blunt, highly ritualized phrases. Minutes after the violent outburst the same siblings will often be found playing happily together, their fury completely forgotten.

Sibling rivalry is indeed normal—the recurring theme of this book—but it changes and varies, ebbs and flows. Where the age gap of your children widens to five, six, or more years, and where the sexes differ, the overlap of their interests is less abrasive. Kids grow up very fast these days, and a five-year gap puts them in worlds that are quite far apart. A seven-year-old girl, going to school, learning to read and skate, busy with her friends and toys, won't have a great deal in common with her two-year-old baby brother. Of course, there will still be competition, particularly for parental attention, and the baby may be considered a "pest" by the older sister, but the tug-of-war is less intense. Here an older sibling is more likely to play the role of sponsor or mentor—and tied in with this is often the urge to control the younger child, to exercise a degree of power.

Besides serving as teacher, an older sib may also act as a young one's protector. Yet, at home the squabbling and fighting go on, but let an outsider try to harm a young sibling, and watch how fast the older one will spring instantly to the rescue! So the reverse side of the rivalry coin is a powerful form of bonding—of great importance to both children.

These teaching-learning relationships are good, but one word of caution: Older sibs, in their eagerness and immaturity, or their need to control, may try to push the younger ones too quickly. Unmindful of a child's limitations, an older brother or sister may have overly high expectations and berate the young sib for not learning quickly enough: "You missed the ball again, you dumbbell!" or "Can't you even balance on a bike?" These and other critical comments only serve to undermine the young one's self-esteem and destroy the benefits of mentoring. So it's a good idea for parents to keep an eye on these situations, to curb the older child's zeal where necessary, and to prevent a young teacher from becoming a young tyrant.

Remember that even when an older sib doesn't play a direct role, he or she will still be a spur to the younger one. Children may not be drawn to emulate the behavior of a mother or father, but will almost inevitably want to have the skills of an older brother or sister, whether it's reading a book, knowing how to swim, playing a computer game, or even getting good marks in school. The drive to emulate an older sibling is incredibly strong and guides much of a young child's actions. Older sibs are natural models, and while this adds to the competition, it also helps younger children to make fast progress in physical and cognitive skills. Envy is a great motivator. The average three-year-old, seeing the accomplishments day in and day out of his five-year-old sibling, will have a strong urge to catch up. So the three-year-old is more likely to be exposed at an earlier point to these various growth stimuli.

Regarding the youngest sib, parents should also note that lastborn kids do tend to be immature and may dislike accepting responsibility. They're often babied and coddled more than the others and aren't taken very seriously. To compensate, the youngest may learn to manipulate—to fret, whine, and cajole in order to get his or her own way.

Your role is to encourage this child's self-reliance and self-respect, praising his or her accomplishments, helping to nurture an all-important sense of growth and progress. At times parents may also have to protect the youngest from harassment. Although siblings are generally patient with the littlest member of the family, some may have to be stopped from always criticizing the young child for being "dumb" or "babyish." But once these minor barriers are overcome, the youngest on the ladder can, like the others, grow into a secure, capable, self-confident adult.

SUMMING UP

The Firstborn Child
- The firstborn is the only one who, for a while, has the parents all to him/herself. Giving up this all-powerful spot when a second baby arrives is a difficult and wrenching experience.
- Since mother and father are new at the game, they may be more anxious and awkward with their first infant than with later ones.
- More is expected of the oldest child. First children tend to be given more duties and responsibilities than the others—sometimes more than they can adequately handle.
- The firstborn is often an achiever. This is in part an attempt to regain the status that had been lost with the second child's arrival.
- Since firstborns have only adults to imitate in the early

years, they tend to be more mature, responsible, and
rule-abiding.

· Due to age and size advantage, the oldest child is often a
leader and usually develops a "take charge" personality,
which helps in achieving success later in life.

· Despite inner strengths, the firstborn is very sensitive
and may secretly feel neglected or pushed aside by the
needs and demands of the younger siblings.

The Second Child

· In two-sib families, rivalry will be most intense where
the age difference is only a few years and where children
are of the same sex.

· The pattern of fighting . . . making up . . . fighting is
normal and doesn't need parental intervention *unless* it
gets violent or excessive.

· Intense, blunt language between siblings doesn't mean
the same thing to them that it does to adults.

· Whereas the older of two sibs has a permanent age advantage, the younger often balances this by shrewd psychological means.

· Where the age gap widens to five years or more, an older
sib may become the younger one's helpful teacher and
mentor—along with the squabbling and the attempts to
control.

· Intended or not, an older sibling inevitably serves as a
healthy spur to growth for the younger one.

The Middle Child

· This child, placed in between, feels pressure from *both*
sides. He or she is neither as privileged as the older sib
nor as pampered as the younger one.

· The middle child's position allows more freedom, since
parental demands and expectations are often less pronounced.

· The middle sib may strive for attention by teasing the
other siblings, breaking family rules and regulations, and
generally acting up.

- The middle child tends to be less conformist and more adventuresome than his or her older sibs. He or she may also have more need for excitement.
- With the example of an older model constantly on hand, middle children feel special pressures. They may respond by trying harder than ever to succeed—or by giving up what appears to be a hopeless struggle.
- The middle child may feel unloved or lacking in self-esteem, a situation that can be corrected by providing extra parental concern and attention.
- A middle child who is the only boy or only girl will have a special sense of uniqueness, which compensates for minor drawbacks in this position.

The Youngest Child

- The youngest on the ladder is often overindulged and overprotected, not only by parents but by the other siblings.
- Since most decisions are made *for* the youngest, who is given little responsibility, this child may tend to be dependent and immature.
- The youngest sib often learns how to manipulate, being bossy or cranky in turn, managing to play one member of the family against another.
- Because he or she may not be taken very seriously, the youngest often feels frustrated and may be lacking in a positive self-image.
- The youngest boy with several older sisters will tend to be relaxed with women and have an easier time relating to them in later life.
- The youngest girl with several older brothers will usually feel secure and comfortable with men and have an easier time relating to them in later life.

CHAPTER

4

Competition—And How to Deal with It

Linda and I knew all about sibling rivalry. We were well prepared, and when the kids came along, we really tried to do all the "right" things. But it didn't seem to help much. They go right on competing and battling!

Parents sometimes feel that knowing about sibling rivalry means they can prevent it. Although parents can and do play a part in easing and modifying conflicts, much of the competition between siblings can't be talked away, wished away, or reasoned away. So the parental role is really to help keep it within reasonable, healthy bounds.

Family specialist Sidonie Gruenberg writes, "Children growing up together continue to be rivals about some things. Competition goes on, now in one form and now in another, along with other kinds of feelings. Each child struggles for his or her place in the family."

The universal struggle of growing children inevitably involves competition; but it's reassuring to know that, within reason, it can be useful and constructive for both child and parent.

THE MANY FACES OF COMPETITION

To begin with, we live in a highly competitive society. Walk through your supermarket and look at the products on the shelves, all vying for consumer dollars. Turn on your TV set. Notice the sports matches—football, baseball, hockey, basketball games—all competitive, all highly popular. Thumb through your favorite newspaper or magazine and notice the ads, which are competing constantly for your attention.

A lot of today's competition involves business and economic goals, but there are other, more subtle kinds. Do you like to play bridge with friends? Do you belong to a bowling league or an office softball team? Want to take some adult courses to sharpen your skills? All these are natural forms of self-expression, and many have a competitive side. Games and contests, mental or physical, do fill a deep human need: They give us pleasure, help to relieve tensions, and offer acceptable ways of expressing aggressive feelings. They also help us to measure and improve our abilities.

Human beings are instinctive achievers; from the beginnings of history, people have tried to better themselves and their world. And although this attempt has not always succeeded, it's what distinguishes us from other species. So the motives behind competition are historic: People do take on challenges in order to solve their problems.

Sometimes the most intense competition is with oneself. A jogger tries to improve his mileage. A salesman seeks to close a bigger deal. A golfer wants to correct his swing, a composer to write a more beautiful melody, an actor to get a rave review. All these strivers, and others, are competing against themselves and their known accomplishments.

Take one well-known example. In May 1953, Sir Edmund Hillary reached the top of the world's highest peak, Mount Everest. When asked why he decided to make the climb, he gave an answer that, though borrowed from an earlier mountaineer, was to become famous: "Because it was there." For Hillary that was reason enough. So, too, all of us try to master our personal Everests, and while our achievements may be less dramatic, the satisfactions are just as real. With every small success, every new accomplishment, we tell ourselves and the world, "I'm somebody."

COMPETITION AND YOUR CHILDREN

On a simpler, more basic level, your youngsters reflect this same striving, for each child, as he or she grows, mirrors the historic urge to improve and do better.

This can be seen in childhood play, which takes different forms and patterns. For toddlers and preschoolers, play usually isn't competitive, but that changes as they approach school age. Here the drive for an identity—*separate and individual*—grows stronger daily, just as small bodies grow stronger. This powerful urge expresses itself in group contests, jump-rope games, jacks and tag, foot races, board games, and card games, such as Old Maid and Concentration. These are important because for kids they're milestones on the long road to physical and mental development. Later, growing children will add organized team sports in which they can pit their strength and skill against their peers.

Watch kids in a playground. Notice how intensely they pursue their games, how fiercely they argue and debate the rules. As they compete, they are in fact modeling themselves on the adult world, feeling their way toward maturity. Experts agree that, as with adults, such activities help children to

· Measure their ability
· Gain new confidence
· Test their capacity to survive and "cope"

Lisa, a ten-year-old, recently sat down to a game of checkers with her favorite uncle. But before the game started, she said, "Uncle Rob, play as hard as you can. Don't just let me win. If you take it easy so I can win, I'll know and I'll get mad." In the past, Lisa wouldn't have minded if her uncle eased up, allowing her to be the winner; but at the age of ten she felt more sure of herself and was eager to test herself against a serious player. For this child, at this point, meeting a fair and honest challenge was really what mattered.

UNHEALTHY COMPETITION

There are, of course, two faces of competitive behavior. One is benign, the other hostile. For most kids competition is a process, not a matter of do-or-die victory. But there can be abuses, in most cases triggered by adult expectations.

We all know the sad stories of aggressive parents who drive their children mercilessly in sports to *win, win, win* at all costs. What this does (aside from giving mom or pop an ego boost) is to create tensions, set unfair standards, and distort a child's normal zest for competitive play. Writer Joanne Oppenheim points out, "When coaches and over-eager parents bring their own competitive yearnings to the ballpark and lay them on the kids, opportunities for learning and enjoyment get squelched." That kind of pressure is not only unfair but can do lasting harm to an impressionable child.

At times, kids also face severe pressure from their peers. Children are vulnerable, and their normal drives—hyped by unrealistic demands of friends and teammates who are bigger, stronger, more skilled—can lead to trouble. For some children, being a team player is a real plus, provided it doesn't pressure them too much or violate personal values and standards.

SOME ALTERNATIVES

Despite the pitfalls, competitive activity, within reason, does help our kids to monitor and measure their growth. It prepares them in many ways for their lives as grown-ups. It can also lead to self-discovery.

- Ten-year-old Mark, physically small and slight, found that he couldn't compete with the bigger kids in rugged contact games, such as football or basketball. But he still had a healthy urge to test his prowess. Encouraged by his parents, Mark soon discovered that he did well in activities where size wasn't important, such as tennis, volleyball, and ice-skating.
- Ginny, a teenager, loved to swim. She tried hard to make her school's swimming team, but didn't quite succeed. However, she fulfilled her goal (and continued her interest in swimming) by becoming the team's assistant manager.

For some children, competition is more mental than physical, and these may develop skill at chess and computer games or in creative fields such as music, writing, and drama. Your child, for example, may really dislike sports, but may welcome the chance to compete in a drawing contest.

These different skill areas aren't mutually exclusive; ideally, your child will develop a good balance between the physical and the mental—which is where you fit in. The parent's role is to be sensitive and understanding, to help channel your own child's competitive drives into those areas where he or she has special interests or ability. But care is needed. Most kids desperately want to please and impress mom and dad, and their antennae are acutely attuned to parental expectations. Mark, the small, slight boy who couldn't compete in contact sports, might be driven to excessive effort because he feels his athletic father would be happy to have a real "jock" for a son. Or a chubby, awkward girl might have similar feelings about pleasing a mother who was a dancer. In both these cases the child's motives become twisted—the urge isn't for self-esteem but for *parental* esteem. The approval of parents is very important, certainly, but not where it leads to distortions; so it's good for parents to keep in mind that it's the child's ego needs—not the adult's—that are involved!

This same clash often exists between siblings, where one has a particular skill that is admired by parents and friends. Here you have to try to help each sibling find and develop his or her own personal strengths and talents, without playing favorites.

Winning and Losing
Competition teaches a child how to play and win, and also how to lose. This last is critical, since all of us, in the course of time, must be able to accept defeat and roll with the punches. Striking a balance between these forces isn't easy. But it can be done when kids develop in an environment where they've seen adults winning and losing with good

grace, and where the *value emphasis* is on playing the game as best one can, rather than on a blind, single-minded drive for victory.

This applies whether competition takes place on the football field or in the creative arena. Most children, like most adults, want success. They're eager to win and anxious to measure up to their peers, and because of this some become perfectionists. Your children need to understand that winning isn't everything—that everyone fails or makes mistakes at times, that a failure or disappointment doesn't signal the end of the world. Kids do learn to cope with the inevitable failures that occur in the normal course of growing up—but support and understanding from a parent can also help to cushion the setbacks.

It also helps to keep your own enthusiasms in perspective. It's natural for a parent to take pride in a child's victories, and a young achiever needs all the support you can muster. But be careful not to lavish exaggerated, unrealistic praise. A child praised excessively, put high on a family pedestal, may come to feel that this is the only thing about himself or herself that is worthy of love.

Special Features of Sibling Competition
Siblings are naturally subject to the same competitive drives as all other children. But when they compete with one another, their methods can take subtle forms. Clare S., age seven, was getting ready for a game of cards with her nine-year-old brother, Peter. Given Peter's age advantage, the outcome seemed foreordained to Clare. Having mulled the problem over, she announced, "Peter, we're going to have a new rule: In this game, the one who comes in second is the winner."

The younger of two siblings is often a manipulator. In this case, Clare, destined by fate to tag forever behind her big brother, at least in age, was simply trying to shorten the odds.

Everything we've seen about competition applies to siblings—only more so! With two or more kids living together under one roof, competitive drives are greatly intensified. Sisters and brothers—especially if close in age and of the same sex—find in each other the perfect partner for competitive battles. Where an only child must seek out friends in school or playground for ritual competition, siblings have built-in rivals right at home, and their contests have many variations. Siblings will compete endlessly over toys and clothes, over who gets the biggest piece of candy, who chooses the TV program, who gets to sit in the front seat of the car. Older siblings give vent to these same needs by competing in games and sports.

All of which is fine when not taken to excess. Plainly and simply, competition between siblings is part of growth, the never-ending struggle to develop a good self-image. A study by the Princeton Center for Infancy states, "A positive self-concept may give a child in later life the courage to 'try' new projects, to accept criticism, to play with ideas; to be creative and venturesome."

Like all forms of competition, sibling competition has plus and minus sides. How can you as a parent encourage the positive aspects and minimize (or eliminate) the negative ones? Let's take a specific look at some basic areas.

Size and Strength
It's not a hard-and-fast rule, but older siblings are usually taller, stronger, more physically adept than their young brothers and sisters; and since kids are intensely conscious of age, size, and physical prowess, this can lead to a mixture of envy and admiration.

As siblings grow, not much can be done about these natural gaps and differences. But parents can be supportive by reassuring the little ones that in time they, too, will be bigger and stronger. This may seem obvious, even trivial, but to a child it's extremely important to be reminded, "Remember how small you were last year? And look how much you've grown since then! Just be patient. Someday you'll be as big as

David." These little reassurances are especially valued at times when an older sibling graduates to a new status level: starting school, getting the first two-wheeler, growing a new tooth, and so on. Trivial, perhaps—but not to a child. Because young children, unlike adults, have a *limited frame of reference* on which to project the future. They really do need to be told what to expect, what to anticipate.

Donna J., a mother of two boys now grown, recalls the early days:

> There's a two-year difference between our kids, and when they were little, a pattern gradually began. Whenever David—he's the oldest—did something big, like starting school or staying overnight at a friend's house, his little brother, Jonathan, would be upset. So he'd climb up on my lap, and I had to tell him that soon *he* would be old enough to do those things. He loved that; I had to do it over and over, saying the same things, which he never got tired of hearing. It seemed to give him reassurance. If *I* said so, it made everything okay.

Older Siblings As Models

In most cases, a younger child will eagerly model his or her skills on the older one. For example, Tim, age twelve, is a body builder who works out with weights. His nine-year-old brother, Phil, admired this and wants to imitate it. Tim can be encouraged to help Phil, starting him out on the easier weights that are appropriate for his age and advising him on what and what not to do. Older kids enjoy this type of mentoring, since it adds to their own fragile confidence. It also helps to strengthen the bond between siblings, a bond that is always there despite surface discords.

Similarly, older siblings can help teach younger ones how to knit, read, ride a bike, throw a football, and so on. Experts find that young children with older models in the family often learn faster and gain new skills more readily—provided they're not pushed beyond their reasonable capacities.

Setting Limits

When siblings compete physically, parents can play a protective role if necessary. It's up to you to make sure that older children don't use their size advantage to bully or harm younger ones. Minor battling and roughhousing are part of the game, but parents must, where necessary, set limits. This is especially true where competition veers toward physical abuse. This can be handled in part by a simple, straightforward rule: "Expressing how you feel is okay. Any time you really get mad, you can come and talk to me about it. I'll always listen. But in this family, there will be no hitting and no violence." Today's social and family rules are broadly permissive, but this shouldn't apply to the kind of physical bullying and intimidation that can lead to psychological problems later on.

Most parents are also familiar with fights in which one child or another will say in a highly injured tone, "But he (or she) started it!" Experts now agree that the answer here is not for a parent to act as judge and jury, trying to sort out all the nuances of guilt or innocence. The origins of sibling squabbles are vague and complex. Did the older child precipitate the fight? Perhaps so. On the other hand, younger siblings do learn how to manipulate, how to goad and provoke older brothers and sisters in various ways. So unless the guilt is clear and blatant, the best course for you is to remain objective and refuse to take sides. Experience shows that the most effective approach is simply to separate the battlers and say as firmly as possible, "It doesn't matter *who* started it. The rule in this family is no hitting. Ever. Period!"

Charles M., a Chicago factory worker, has a brother three years older than himself. He still remembers the battles:

John and I shared a room, and there was a lot of rivalry between us. I was a pretty big kid, almost as big as John, and from the time I was about eight, the quarrels would get violent. Real battles—fistfights, wrestling, the works. My father didn't want to squelch our "manly" instincts, so he usually tried to be the go-between. You know, to keep us within bounds. But it began to get very bad, so finally he made a new rule: No matter who was to blame, or how it got started, if we began any hard fighting, we *both* got punished. They were tough punishments, too—we were deprived of something we really wanted to do, going to a movie or a ball game or something. So with *that* hanging over us, we toned down—had to find other ways to handle our problems.

If the battles start up again despite warnings, one solution is to put the fighters in separate rooms, to keep them apart until they calm down. At this point you can also threaten punishment should hostilities resume—loss of a privilege, or cancellation of a planned outing. Remember that, at this crucial stage, the family unit is a sibling's "society-at-large." What your children learn at home about values and personal behavior will be carried through life and into the outside world. So it's essential to make clear that while competition is okay, violence, whether hitting, punching, biting, kicking are simply not allowed.

Violence can also take verbal forms. Vicious, cruel name-calling can be as harmful at times as physical blows and can be ruled out just as firmly. Of course you can't monitor everything your siblings say to each other, but when vicious language occurs in your hearing, don't hesitate to put a stop to it—and to have the name-caller apologize on the spot.

Child psychologist Selma Fraiberg writes, "It seems to me that we have to draw the line in sibling rivalry whenever rivalry goes out of bounds into destructive behavior of a physical or verbal kind. The principle needs to be this: Whatever the reasons for your feelings, you will have to find civilized solutions."

Sports and Games
In a more structured way, competition underlies games and sports. Again, since an older sibling will have an advantage over the younger, the older child can be encouraged to be the young one's coach. When an older child teaches and a youn-

ger one learns, a rich give-and-take develops, markedly helpful to both. But here again care and judgment are called for:
Don't let an older sib set excessive, unfair standards for the
younger ones.

Also, jeers and put-downs by an older brother or sister can
undermine the younger one's confidence. Human feelings are
universal; even the toughest-skinned sibling will be harmed
by bullying and taunting. A young child ridiculed too often
by an older sibling may become timid, withdraw from the
competitive arena, and hesitate to try new ventures.

- One little girl, eight-year-old Marcy, was an avid baseball
  fan and was eager to learn how to play, but her ten-year-old
  brother wanted no part of it. Proud of his own skill as a
  budding player, he taunted his little sister, made fun of her
  efforts, and reminded her repeatedly that she'd never be a
  good player because she was "only a girl."
- John, a star on his high school football team, was anxious to
  teach the game to his younger brother, Andy. In a mis-
  guided effort to "toughen" his kid brother, he insisted on
  tackling the boy as hard as he tackled his bigger high school
  opponents. Andy not only suffered physically but had to
  bear John's taunts that he couldn't "take it." Not surprisingly, this turned the young sib off, and made him timid
  about all contact sports.

Needless to say, this insidious kind of ridicule and pressure
will be harmful and should be stopped. Taunts and jeers are a
form of verbal violence and have to be rejected.

TO INTERFERE OR NOT TO INTERFERE?

Sometimes, to reiterate, it's best for parents *not* to interfere in
sibling squabbles. Squabbling does help kids to work out
day-to-day problems on their own—and they're usually successful at doing so.

When brothers and sisters play together and compete, they

generally set up rules and regulations to their own satisfaction. This helps them act out social rules and polish their skills at communicating with one another. Setting rules, then arguing over them, then refining them, is normal for young competitors. There's no need for a parent to interfere unless specifically called on to settle a dispute—and here again, fairness is the watchword.

Of course, you'll have to interfere if things get out of hand and deteriorate into physical violence. But often, sensitive parents can anticipate blowups; they get to know the telltale signs that inevitably lead to unacceptable behavior.

For instance, Alan M. knew that his eight-year-old teased her younger sister when she mispronounced certain words. (The younger one got a lot of attention from adults, who thought these mispronunciations were cute.) Alan also knew that the younger one would tolerate the teasing just so long, then would hit her sister, and a full-fledged battle would begin. It only took a couple of unhappy incidents before Alan was able to see what was coming and nip it in the bud. He tried several approaches. At first he told his older daughter that he didn't like her teasing the younger one and that this wouldn't be tolerated any longer. Then he went a step further. He tried distracting the older child with another activity. Since the subject was words, Alan suggested a simple word game that involved guessing meanings, then looking them up in the dictionary. The game proved successful—and of interest to both the kids. What Alan did in effect was to offer a positive alternative, at the same time reinforcing the no-teasing rule. *Anticipation* coupled with *distraction* is a technique worth trying in situations where siblings squabble repeatedly over the same predictable issue.

At times, in family games, you might also try a little handicapping. In a foot race a younger child might be given some extra yardage as a head start. In a game of checkers, the older sib can start with one or two fewer pieces. Here again, care should be exercised: An older child, constantly required to give an advantage to the younger, may develop a lot of resentment and feel that the young one is the family favorite.

In general, it's best to encourage your siblings to compete most of the time with their peers outside the family. When children play games with others in their own age bracket, many of these touchy areas are avoided; the kids themselves can compete in a natural and satisfying manner, testing their growing bodies and skills against their equals.

SOCIAL/CULTURAL COMPETITION

As adults we're familiar with the personality traits of friends and relatives: Charlie is the quiet, solid type; Myra the good storyteller; Henry is shy and retiring; Ellen the life of the party. Similarly among kids, different traits begin to emerge—and at a surprisingly early age. According to child-care expert Dr. Benjamin Spock, "Many of the patterns of personality are quite clear by two or three years of age." This doesn't mean that kids won't go on changing; as we've seen, change is constant and inevitable as kids encounter new challenges and react to new experiences. But as their individual traits appear, these may become part of the rivalry game.

The assets of a growing child are physical, social, mental, and creative. All these strengths contribute to a child's status and self-esteem, and can be used competitively. In short, physical rivalry is only one of the ways in which siblings satisfy the urge to compete with one another.

· Seven-year-old Sally can't hold her own very successfully in athletic contests with her ten-year-old sister. But she discovers that she has a rather lively sense of humor and a knack for telling funny stories. Sally soon becomes the family jokester, amusing everyone at the dinner table as well as her friends and classmates.

· Larry, age twelve, feels inadequate when it comes to physical competition, partly because his older brother is a sports hero in school. But Larry has a talent for writing. He starts a class newspaper, and with it he organizes a school scrap drive. This gives Larry the status and satisfaction that elude him on the playing field.

· Nine-year-old Harriet can't throw a ball properly. Physically she's a bit clumsy and takes a lot of teasing from her older siblings, who are more athletically inclined. But Harriet is a good student; she concentrates on her schoolwork, does well, even begins to win scholastic competitions. This impresses her siblings and gives Harriet a needed ego boost.

Children may find outlets as artists or actors, dancers or musicians. Some discover that they're adept with their hands and take up crafts and hobbies. Others develop interests in science, math, or astronomy. And some, like Harriet, may invest much of their energy in school projects. Obviously, these interests aren't mutually exclusive—a good ball player can also be a top student, a skilled swimmer an avid musician, and so on. These abilities are all part of an expanding world—natural outlets for curiosity and creativity—and as such need your full encouragement.

In sum, kids are pioneers, constantly testing capabilities and marching toward personal horizons. But sometimes a newly acquired social or creative skill can serve as a subtle tool in the competitive arena. This, too, is normal, as long as these traits aren't distorted or used self-destructively.

Where Do You Come In?
As a parent of siblings, your job is to provide a balance, to apply common sense where needed, to try to keep certain patterns from becoming "runaways." From time to time, you might ask yourself, "Is this new interest (or skill or talent) becoming obsessive? Is it being used only as compensation—something for her or him to hide behind?"

Let's look at our examples and speculate:

· Sally, the family humorist, overdoes her knack for joke telling. In order to stay in the spotlight, she becomes the school clown. As Sally grows older, she begins to feel that acceptance by her siblings and peers depends upon her always playing the buffoon.

- Larry, the writer, enjoys his newfound status as a newspaper editor. This has many rewards—and legitimate ones. But Larry goes too far, spends all his time on newspaper activities, and seriously neglects his regular schoolwork. Though bright and competent, his investment of time and energy is thrown out of balance.
- Harriet, the good student, uses her school grades as compensation for her athletic shortcomings. She begins slowly to withdraw from other normal childhood games and activities, buries herself in her books, and is on her way to becoming a lonely school drudge.

With each of these kids a normal drive has taken a self-destructive turn, and some parental intervention is in order. But the watchword again is "handle with care." Most experts agree that, with siblings, parents should interfere as little as possible, and only when such intervention is necessary and can be truly helpful. They also agree that some parents tend to worry excessively and overreact to their children's transient problems. But when your input is called for, remember that it should be timely and tactful.

Sally, Larry, Harriet—our sample siblings—have a lot in common. Basically unsure of themselves, they struggle to be accepted and admired for something they can do, rather than for who they are. Though this is a classic, fairly common attitude, it can be tempered by loving and understanding parents: EVERY CHILD NEEDS TO KNOW THAT HE OR SHE IS WORTHY OF RESPECT AS AN INDIVIDUAL, REGARDLESS OF SPECIFIC GIFTS, SKILLS, OR TALENTS. This can be achieved both by words and actions and by the attention you pay to each of your siblings as an individual, valued person.

Some children may also need help in broadening their interests. A particular talent is important, but ought not to be pursued to the exclusion of all other activities. Children do need guidance; and here your intuitive knowledge of your own child, plus your patience and tact, can help.

Today's parents and children are far more able to communicate than in earlier generations; feelings can be discussed and problems aired with greater freedom than ever before. So don't hesitate to talk frankly with a sibling when the need arises. If a child develops an obsession with a new interest or hobby and totally ignores other matters, you can sit down with her or him and discuss it. You don't have to be a practicing psychologist for this; simply apply your own loving common sense. Ask questions, draw out your child's thoughts, make constructive suggestions. You might say, for instance, "We think your sketchbook is terrific. You're getting to be a super artist, and we're very proud of you. But aren't you neglecting your schoolwork? From now on, why not do all your homework first? Then you'll have free time to put in on your drawings." Or, "We haven't seen Jay around here for a while. Those ship models are really beautiful—but, you know, you've been kind of neglecting your friends. Why not call and invite Jay to have dinner with us tomorrow? Afterward you can work on your models together."

Pinning Labels

We all know parents who hang tags on their kids: "He's the bookworm of the family" or "She's the smart one" or "He's the clumsy one—Mr. All Thumbs." There are also "the clown," "the shy type," "the slow learner," "the TV actress," "the worrier," and so on. Whereas adults may use these terms half in jest, children tend to take them seriously. Labeling can be risky, since it helps to reinforce a child's own self-concept, often in a harmful way. A youngster who's constantly tagged at home as clumsy or sloppy or a slow learner will tend to become even more so. In this sense, the label becomes self-fulfilling prophecy.

Ten-year-old Linda was known in her family as Miss Klutz.

Whenever Linda stubbed a toe, knocked over a glass of milk, or—on rare occasions—dropped a dish in the kitchen, her older siblings would chorus gleefully, "There goes 'klutzy' again!" Subconsciously, Linda began to accept this role and live up to expectations. But her parents, sensitive to the problem, quietly put a stop to the teasing. They also made a point of complimenting Linda when she did something that showed dexterity, such as fixing a broken toy or sewing on a missing button, which gradually helped to change her self-image.

Not all labels are negative, of course, but even the complimentary ones are risky. A child who's constantly referred to as the "family genius" finds himself or herself carrying a heavy burden. Eager to please proud parents and live up to their opinions, the youngster may try too hard and develop real anxieties about schoolwork. Bringing home a less-than-perfect grade can thus become a painful and unnecessary trauma.

Making Comparisons
"Look at your sister's room. Why can't you be neat and tidy like her?"

"Are you going to be as smart in school as your big brother?"

"She has beautiful hair, but her sister's is stringy."

"He got the looks in the family, and she got the brains."

We all hear comments like these, or ones very similar. On the physical side, parents will compare siblings' eyes, hair, complexion, size, and strength. Other comparisons may deal with children's talents, schoolwork, behavior, and personality traits.

Of course it's hard for parents to avoid comparisons, but this kind of verbal game carries pitfalls, especially when comparisons are made in the child's hearing. A child's main job is to grow up whole, and the parent's role is to help and encourage this. But a parent who constantly makes comparisons creates obstacles to the process, because when one makes a comparison, one is actually making a judgment, in which one party usually suffers.

Making comparisons, whether good or bad, is a more elaborate form of labeling; and like labels, comparisons carry messages that are quickly picked up by youngsters. In a family of two siblings, in which one is constantly praised for looks, brains, or behavior in contrast to the other, the low man on the totem pole will draw obvious conclusions: that he or she is *lacking* in these praiseworthy qualities. The favored sibling may become vain, while the neglected one feels resentment and envy and in time may get discouraged and give up trying to improve.

A well-meaning parent might say, for instance, "She's always well-behaved, but her little sister is a menace." While this could be true, verbalizing it only reinforces the younger child's negative feelings about herself and further fuels the ever-present fires of sibling rivalry. Making comparisons is a no-win situation and should be avoided by parents concerned for their children's healthy development. Keep in mind that each child is different and develops in his or her own unique way. A little sister can certainly be told that she is a "menace" if her actions warrant it, but it's gratuitous and even damaging also to include that the older sister is a perfect, well-behaved jewel. When you compare your kids excessively, you may be labeling one of them a loser.

"IT'S MINE!" "NO, IT'S MINE!"

Toys . . . clothes . . . games . . . candy bars . . . sports equipment . . . you name it, siblings will wrangle over it. Nothing sparks a quarrel between sisters and brothers quite as quickly, or as intensely, as competition over possessions, things that—because they're visible and tangible—become easy pawns in the ongoing rivalry.

Siblings close in age will squabble over clothes; and all will battle over toys, games, books, and the prerogatives of ownership, including that inevitable "biggest piece of cake."

Actually, most of this quarreling is *neither mindless nor irrational,* but plays a role in sibling development. Child psychologists tell us that squabbling between sibs isn't merely a necessary evil or an aberration that parents have to tolerate. Squabbling isn't a way kids have of simply killing time. In actual fact, it's the way they discover their capacities and work out their relationships with other human beings. They grow emotionally through these processes, not in spite of them.

Underlying this is the fact that a very young child's identity is closely tied to certain objects and possessions. One of the earliest notions of self-discovery picked up by a child is the concept of "mine" and "yours." This is closely linked to an even more basic sense of "me" as distinguished from "you." A toddler of less than two years already possesses this instinct for "what is mine." To the toddler, clothes, a pull-toy, or a beloved stuffed animal is literally part of himself or herself. The child's sense of *identity* is strongly linked to the *object.* But toddlers aren't yet aware of other people's rights, so they will help themselves freely to any appealing bauble or toy belonging to another. Later on, as children reach three or four years of age, the idea of ownership is more clearly understood, and they now begin to recognize some of the rights of others to personal possessions.

Here a parent's job is to protect each child's rights, to monitor disputes, to see that possessions are used and apportioned fairly. The concept of fairness is important to siblings, especially where possessions are involved. In other words, it's better to say, "I know this doll is yours—but could you let your little sister play with it, just for a while?" than arbitrarily to take an older sibling's property and hand it to a younger one.

Similarly, the older and bigger sibling shouldn't be allowed to appropriate a younger one's things without the sibling's agreement. This seems almost too obvious to mention, but the most obvious things (for that very reason) are often taken for granted. It's good to remember that a young child has very few props to his or her sense of self, and one important prop is an attachment to certain possessions. When this "identity attachment" is ignored, when rights are carelessly brushed aside by parents or siblings, jealousy and resentment can be the result.

A child's belongings are an extension of the child—and that includes the freedom to use and enjoy them. In family living, accepting this helps to build mutual respect. Let's say, for instance, that a four-year-old spends a lot of time laboring happily over a big construction of blocks with a friend. Then along comes a two-year-old sibling, who knocks the whole thing to the floor without a moment's thought. Natural enough for a two-year-old, but we all know the familiar howls of indignation that will result! In this case, it isn't enough to remind the older sibling that his or her baby brother or sister is "too young to understand." The point is worth making, but it should be accompanied by steps to protect the older child from the younger one's unthinking actions. Siblings, regardless of age or place in the family, have to know that their rights will be guarded and protected; this, in turn, teaches them how to respect the needs and rights of others.

This is not to say that belongings are to be treated as sacred. In this materialistic society, possessions are often given too much importance. But the principle still remains valid: Each of your siblings has his or her right of ownership, and dealing with competition in this area is largely a matter of fair treatment and parental common sense.

Age Differences
As your siblings grow, their age levels also play a part in patterns of ownership and should be clearly acknowledged. It helps siblings to learn and accept that they can't always have everything their brothers or sisters have. As one mother of four kids put it, "Not every child's shoes wear out at the same time." Part of a child's maturing is seeing that indeed there are differences in age and size, and that this carries with

it some prerogatives. Not every sibling will be ready at the same time for a school bag, ice skates, or a ten-speed bike. Here it's basically a matter of reassuring the one who's left out with, "You're not ready for school yet, but when you start school, you'll get one, too," or "Bobby's big enough now to manage a two-wheeler, but it would be a little risky for you. Just be patient; we'll get you one later, when you're Bobby's age." In addition, a parent can point out to the younger sibling the exciting and interesting things he or she is ready for, right now.

The pattern continues with older siblings, where one may be old enough for a learner's permit to drive a car or ready to start guitar or violin lessons. Again, the younger kids have to be reminded that parents aren't playing favorites, that it's a question of age and time, and that their turn will come.

To Share or Not to Share
Much is made these days of the need for sharing. Families are urged, rightly enough, to share everything, from sports, museum visits, outings, and TV programs to ideas, thoughts, and feelings. Among siblings, certain possessions can also readily be shared—a basketball, an inflatable swimming raft, a badminton set or Scrabble game. Sibling sisters, preteen and older, very often enjoy sharing clothes and costume jewelry—though not without squabbles! Here it's good to keep the importance of identity in mind. Sharing is important, but only up to a point; when possible, kids are generally better off with their own individual belongings, recognized and identified as such.

By giving siblings clear title to their own belongings, we encourage responsibility and respect for others, and at the same time cut down on competition. We also give them a feeling of control.

Two young brothers, for example, shared a large room and a bulletin board. The kids loved their bulletin board, but it became a constant source of friction, since each boy wanted space for his own prized photos, notes, buttons, and so on.

The solution was simple and obvious: two bulletin boards, each with the child's name on top, for each to use and decorate as he chose. Does this mean you always have to provide two of everything? No—but often, with small things, it's a good solution. If your siblings are close in age and the family budget will allow, duplicate purchases of smaller items are a wise idea, since it creates a sense of fairness and helps eliminate jealous wrangling.

Competition can also be minimized if each sibling has his or her own physical place where prized possessions are kept. This can be any area where a child's belongings can be stored. Things of one's own require a place of one's own, which also encourages kids to develop a sense of responsibility. This personal space doesn't have to be enormous, since its value is partly symbolic. If your space is limited, you can divide a closet, assign certain drawers in a chest, put a toy box in a corner or in a hall—do whatever is necessary to create this precious private place, no matter how modest.

Having a special area to keep belongings is part of a sibling's self-identity. It symbolizes his or her own special place in the family's scheme of things. So don't be upset if your siblings, who may share the same room, divide it carefully into "your half" and "my half." To you this may seem strange or silly, but to the kids involved it's a serious matter, a way of asserting their individuality. Sharing is important for growing children; but so are those highly prized rights of ownership.

Along with ownership rights goes the need for privacy—as precious for growing children as it is for their parents. It may not be possible or practical to provide each of your siblings with his or her own room, but they *can* be given certain areas, and certain times, where their personal privacy is respected. Kids, always under the sharp eyes of their elders, do need their own small retreats and their own small secrets. A diary with a lock on it, a tree house, some private corner in the attic, a makeshift "clubhouse" in the back yard—all these are important to your siblings. And necessary, too. For these all symbolize to youngsters their very own "turf," places where they can play, read, think, dream—and enjoy the right to be themselves.

CHAPTER 5

Parents Talk about Competition

Speaking of competition, how much is really "normal" between siblings? There's no precise way to determine this, since every family is different; much depends on the children involved, the nature of the family, the age and temperament of each sibling. Some kids are more combative and assertive than others, some are more placid and easygoing, and these basic psychological variations all play a part.

In some families the rivalry is fairly moderate, but in many cases, and at certain stages, it can be intense. There are as many variations as there are human personalities. However, the competition is generally present in one form or another, and certainly isn't always easy to live with! But it does seem to be inevitable; it has a valid purpose, and in time much of it dissipates.

As you read the comments of the following typical parents, keep in mind that they're talking about average youngsters who are trying hard to maintain a tenuous footing on their own bumpy paths to growth and maturity.

Frank M., father of Jeffrey, age seven, and Linda, age eleven: "I don't recall when the competition really raised its head, but we're right in the middle of it now. I'll tell you, it's unbelievable. They're at each other all the time. Or most of the time. It's amazing to me the amount of counting that Jeffrey—that's the younger one—the amount of counting he does, and the detail he notices; the way he measures everything and checks to see whether Linda is getting more than he is. You name it: whether it's food on his plate, minutes to watch TV, time allowed for staying up, or times their grandparents have taken them out on some sort of special occasion. He keeps track of it all. . . .

"My sense is that Jeffrey's world is very powerfully defined by Linda's presence. She is definitely a major figure in his world. I think that's far more true than he would ever admit, and I think she knows it and that it's far more powerful than she would admit. But she does know she's got this kind of a power, in a sense, being his big sister. He would do anything to have her favor and approval. . . .

"It's a difficult problem. Sometimes they come to us—Nancy and me—to settle a quarrel, and we find ourselves constantly looking for the perfect standard of fairness to apply. But there are times, depending on the pressures Nancy and I are feeling, when it gets to be too much. The world is not always fair. So we make an arbitrary decision and that's that, and they've just got to live with it.

"In most cases we try to do a little fact-finding, because the first rule is that, whatever one is told, one can't always believe only one side of a story. There's always another side to the grievance. We also try to get them to settle disputes with each other and to talk it over with each other. That's a principle that we try to follow, but we find that it's really hard to make it work. We do have to intervene a lot more than we want to, but I think they're not old enough yet—not at a stage where they can work all these things out between themselves.

"Here's a specific example: Sunday-night TV. One of our rules is that they take turns. They're allowed to watch TV for one hour a night, and they each take turns picking their programs. On Sunday nights they alternate because he likes to watch one show, and she likes to watch another. Jeffrey had just started watching a program when Linda walked into the living room and just started switching the channel. Jeff immediately burst into tears and came crying to us that it wasn't fair, that it was his turn. She then said that she was just looking. I mean, Linda knew it wasn't right, she was just in there to annoy him. Well, we had to find out whose turn it really was, had to learn who had watched what the previous week, and so on. It was in fact Jeffrey's turn at the set, and we were strong in telling her that she wasn't being fair, that she was, in fact, just being mean to her brother.

"I don't know that it solved anything, but it did give him the feeling that we were supporting him in an instance when she was in the wrong. In a sense, that's a lot of what we do. We very much want them to stick up for themselves and work things out—but we also want them to know that we'll stick up for each of them. That we won't turn our backs. . . .

"Another recent incident comes to mind. My in-laws came for a visit about two months ago and took Linda out for a special day—and it was really funny because Jeff didn't say anything about it. I didn't even know he realized what was happening, that they were taking her out and so on. That day he went and played with a friend and there wasn't a peep out of him. About three weeks later, in one of those conversations about 'what's fair' and 'who gets what,' he brought it up: '*She's* the one who gets to go out with Gramps and Nana. She's the one who gets all those special treats.' So he was quietly logging in this differential! Of course, we had told him they were coming for another visit soon, and then it would be his turn to have a special day with them. But it's interesting, he's now at this 'age of reason,' and he logs in these precedents like a lawyer. He can cite times and places where the family has been 'unfair' and where he thinks he hasn't gotten his due. He's not right, but he does harbor these vague grievances. I have this sense that each of them, no matter what we do, carries around this idea that we give special treatment to the other. Jeffrey feels it more than Linda does. He's very sensitive to the fact that, well—she's allowed to go to the supermarket by herself to buy things; she's allowed to take the bus by herself to go to school; and so on.

"Basically, what bothers him is simply that she's got the edge. That she's always going to be older and will always get to do things before he can. Of course we can reassure him and point out that he'll do those things later when he's big enough. But he's not satisfied. He immediately wants to know, well—what's Linda going to be able to do then? I guess the main struggle with him is to get him to accept the fact that he's not her, that she's four years older, and four years does make a difference. What we want him to feel is that he is, in fact, a very capable, very terrific seven-year-old. But that a seven-year-old is still not an eleven-year-old. And that's the hardest thing to do—but I know it's mostly a matter of time. And patience.

"What advice could I give other parents? I guess I would say, Listen to your kids and try to be fair. And don't worry if you can't always solve everything, if the problem seems too difficult. I think I've become more comfortable with my own arbitrariness and my need at times just to say, 'I'm sorry, but that's the way it is.' In other words, I know I can set limits to my involvement—not to feel that to be a good parent I always have to have endless discussions with my kids. I try to listen actively, but there comes a point where I do have to draw the line somehow—which probably has more to do with me than with them. Also, if Nancy or I have been unfair with them, we admit it, so that they'll know we can make mistakes, that we're not oracles. They know clearly that we're the authorities, but we're not invincible.

"I'll say one thing—sometimes the kids do get along beautifully. They'll play together for a while or go swimming together when we're at the beach. At times like those, they really enjoy each other, love each other. It doesn't happen very often, but when it does, it's magic."

Susan L., mother of Amy, age seven, and Peter, age twelve: "In our family, the rivalry didn't really start until our kids got older. The first few years were uneventful. There's a five-year difference between them, and Peter was pretty pleased with having Amy, and she didn't impinge on his life very much. But it did start up later, and what Mark and I have finally come to realize is that in our family, any family, living together in a family is learning to fight as well as learning to love. It seems to be woven together.

"Another thing is I think that in a way some parents have an unconscious bias that depends, as much as anything, on whether a child reminds them of themselves or not. Qualities that remind us of something we wish we had. Or didn't have. It colors our thinking. So for a parent to deal with sibling rivalry, I think it's really important to know what your bias is, and whether it's fair or not.

"In our family, there's a typical pattern to the sibling fights, which is to say that Amy, our seven-year-old, usually starts them. In my work, my interviews with parents, I often find that it's the younger ones that start the squabbling, and often they start them in a devious, kind of sneaky way. They'll say or do something deliberately; then the older child will explode. Of course families do differ in who starts the fight—but with Amy, she sometimes wants to get Peter in trouble. If life is boring, or she's tired, or hungry, and a little scrap will spice things up, she'll pick on him. Usually she'll do something that's pretty innocuous, like eating with her mouth open or mispronouncing his name. Or she'll say he's got 'baby pudge.' He's turning twelve, and about to shoot up in height, and he's suddenly gotten a little heavier, so she'll tease him about getting fat or something, but in a quiet way. Then BOOM, he'll react and do something worse to her than the little teasing she did. Yank her hair hard, for instance. Then he gets into trouble, and Amy sits back with her arms folded and enjoys it. Mark and I finally caught on to the pattern, and now we get Amy to quit—we handle it in terms of the way the fight really started.

"My bias was always to protect Amy, because she reminds me of myself and because she's so much smaller than Peter. I was also the smallest. But Peter reminds me of my bad temper, so I don't like to see him explode. Too close to home, I guess. . . .

"Well, he and I have sat down and had some 'strategy' talks about this. I say, 'Hey, Peter, you know, you shouldn't let her get to you. You should figure out that she's baiting you, trying to start something—and you always lose because then you pull her hair or hit her, or do something worse than the teasing. So you wind up in trouble. You've got to figure out a way to handle this with her.' I keep saying, 'She's laying traps for you. It's like an animal trap in the woods; don't step in it!' Well, he's gotten better at not taking the bait, not saying, 'You're this, or you're that.' Instead of an 'I' message he delivers a 'you' message, like 'When you tease me, Amy, I don't like it. So just stop.'

"Believe it or not, it's been working! I think what I'm trying to do with Peter in this little situation is give him a good strategy to cope with it. The kind of strategy that he may also be able to use as an adult. Maybe it will help him to avoid other traps later on. . . .

"Of course we talk to Amy, too. Usually there's an underlying grievance. Something that he did earlier, something that happened that bothered her, and the teasing is her way of dealing with it. It's her way of getting back. So I've been encouraging her to confront him, to tell him directly what he did that she didn't like. We also have family meetings—we have rules about how these are run—and it's a chance for everyone to air their problems. This is where Amy can get things off her chest. Where we all can. It's been very helpful.

"They compete in other ways, sure. They compete over skills. Amy is five years younger, and in most things Peter is more competent. He can do things that she doesn't ever think she'll be able to do. Like she'll see him doing really hard school reports, or speaking French now. Or physical things—you know, really slamming a baseball. On the other hand, Peter has had math problems, and Amy is getting very competent in math. And he doesn't like it one single bit that she's as advanced as he is already! I mean, he was learning some very simple math facts at the end of last year that she, five years younger, is handling already. Also, Amy is a real reader. She started a Judy Blume book—she's seven—yesterday, and she finished reading it this morning in the car. It was about 140 pages, and she read it straight through. Now Peter only read that book last year. He's capable of reading, but he's not the kind of bookworm that she seems to be. So he sees her sitting there with her face in a book that he has only recently read, and she's laughing and enjoying it, and I think he feels jealous and competitive with her about that. He'll come over then and say something like, 'Your friends never call you. I've gotten three calls today, and nobody's called to play with you.' I mean, he'll come out with a little remark to put her down. When Amy looks like she's catching up to Peter, she finds it immensely satisfying, but somehow Peter finds it extraordinarily unnerving. . . .

"I know there are some families that say their kids don't fight, and love each other all the time, but I think in most families there is squabbling. I mean, think about anybody you live with—I've had moments of being jealous of Mark, and Mark has had moments of being jealous of me. In a close family, you just open yourself up; you feel all the feelings that human beings feel: love, hate, anger, compassion, joy, sorrow, jealousy, rage. You know, all those feelings. And I think my hope for my kids is that, within the family, they can learn positive and constructive ways for dealing with all those emotions. Mark and I don't fight much, but occasionally when we do have a dispute, we don't try to hide it from the kids. I've always thought that it's a good example for them—to see that their parents can have a scrap and still love each other very much. They're honest fights. Neither of us calls each other names, we each say what we're feeling, and we try to work it out. Then it's out, it's over, and it's not violent. . . .

"In general, depending on the way your siblings are spaced, there are plusses and minuses. In my case, the fact that I have a boy and a girl who are five years apart—there probably will never be a whole lot they'll like to do in common. So they may never be the kind of close friends of my own childhood idyllic memory. On the other hand, you never know. Sometimes it's a good idea to take them away from their everyday circumstances and put them together with each other, and you find (at least we found when we took a family vacation together with just our two kids) that, with all the rest of society stripped away, they really had a wonderful time together. They swam together, they had a very good time with each other, they played games, they read to each other, they even liked listening to the same books when Mark or I read to them. Basically, we feel very good about our kids' relationships with each other; we try to help them with the competition, but we accept it as part of their growing up."

Walter C., father of Abigail, age nine; Gary, age twelve; and Patricia, age fourteen: "For a long time the rivalry was mostly between my two oldest, Gary and Patricia, but over the years it has shifted. Now it's Gary and Abigail who do the squabbling. There are three and a half years between them—and at fourteen, Patricia is pretty well established as her own person. She's feeling more secure now in herself, but the other two are pretty much embroiled with each other.

"Interestingly, they don't compete over the big, important things, just the little things: card games, Monopoly, candy, who gets to sit in the front seat of the car, and so on. The children live with their mother during the week, about sixty miles from here. They're with me most weekends—say, two out of three weekends—though these days Patty may have plans and arrangements of her own. Usually I pick them up in the car Friday afternoon or evening, and bring them back on Sunday night. That long ride is very important to us—a time when we're together without television or books or games or distractions, such as going to the store or answering the phone. It's kind of a crucible—I mean, you're really there, and nobody can just walk away from it. . . .

"The car ride is really a good time for us all. We might play games or listen to the radio a little. But often we like to talk, we talk seriously about things on our minds. Maybe things we've been saving up all week. And yes, to this day there's still competition about who gets to sit in front! It's by far the preferred seat; the person who sits in front really gets to do more talking with me than the other people. Usually the kids take turns at this, unless somebody has a special or serious problem—then that gets priority.

"My kids get along well with each other, but that doesn't mean there isn't rivalry. It seems to be a built-in part of their lives. It's going to be the candy they buy on the weekend or the comic book or the TV program or who gets the big chair—you can't set up a situation where there's not going to be that kind of squabbling!

"Partly, I think, it's because a family is a group of people who are living together in rather intense situations. The group will always be a family; and no matter how the dynamics may change, the kids will always be brothers and sisters, relating to each other on this very intense level. I think that right from the time the second child is born, there's a natural, built-in rivalry. When the mother is pregnant, that second child 'has' the mother's body. And when the baby is born, it takes a piece of the parents, you might say, which the first one had all to himself in the beginning. I'm not saying children would ever articulate this, nor would I want them to, but it is a fact of life. . . .

"When my kids bicker, I try not to interfere—it isn't usually that important. *Unless* they begin to get violent. I remember a time when Patty ran at Gary to scratch him, and I shoved her away hard, not just to protect him but because I was angry at her. There's nothing more difficult for a parent, I think, than to see one of their children hurt. That's terribly painful for a parent, and when one of your kids is really hurting the other, it's impossible to remain detached. But we do have a strong rule about 'no violence,' which they do usually stick to.

"There's one other thing I'd like to mention—maybe it's because I'm a teacher and I'm more aware of this—but kids don't use language the way we adults do. There's really a big difference. One of the things I see happening in my class of four- and five-year-olds is that the children will often say, 'I hate you!' or 'I'll never talk to you again,' usually over some very minor matter. But ten minutes later they're the best of friends. Adults don't function that way. If I said to an adult, 'You're very stupid; I despise you,' or 'You're really obnoxious,' it would be serious—there would be a complete, total break. No shaking hands a few minutes later. But kids get over this kind of assault almost immediately, and I think that's good for parents to realize. It helps to keep in mind that kids do use language differently than we adults and aren't affected in the same way adults are by that kind of rivalry.

"I know that's hard for parents to accept. In a way, I think it's easier for me, because I see it happening every day in my classroom, and I know it so well. . . .

"Another thing I try to remember is that when the kids squabble or compete over something, they're not just passing time—they're actually polishing up their skills, their negotiating skills. Learning how to deal with others. So I think it's important for parents to say sometimes, 'You two are old enough to work it out for yourselves. I'll sit and listen to the two of you, but you have to sit and talk to each other and try to find a solution.'

"It also helps to spot certain patterns. The rivalry doesn't matter so much to Patricia anymore. As I say, she's older now and feeling pretty secure in herself. But Gary and Abigail are still at it. The pattern here is that Abby, the youngest, will set up situations where Gary, the twelve-year-old, will tease her; and she encourages the teasing, encourages the rivalry, to a point where it gets critical, and then comes running to me for protection. It's very hard for her to see, to understand, that it's really she who is the 'passive aggressor,' to use an interesting term. Abby can manipulate the situation and look like she's the victim, when in fact she has set it all up. For instance, she might come to me sobbing that Gary won't get off her bed, when she has really invited him, cajoled him, to sit on the bed—and then pushed him into a situation where he can't get off the bed without losing face or something. My first instinct, of course, is to say to Gary, 'Get off her bed, leave her alone, stop teasing her,' and scold him, when it's really Abby who started the whole business.

"It's tricky, and there are no easy, pat answers to these things. Parents just have to remember that each of their kids is a different kind of person. With differing temperaments, also differing needs. No one can predict all the time how siblings might behave or react, but it's all part of family living. I think what parents need to do is to look very carefully at their children. Look at them as individuals. Listen to them; they'll usually tell you where they're at, what they need from you. That's one of my main personal themes: Children will tell you—if you listen closely to them."

CHAPTER
6

—And Baby Makes Four

I'm six months pregnant and our three-year-old, Nancy, hasn't said or noticed anything yet. Tom and I are wondering, when do we break the news to her? Exactly what should we say? If she seems jealous or upset, how do we handle it?

Four-year-old Robert was a demanding and willful child, so his parents were naturally worried about how he'd react to a new sibling in the house. Of course, Robert had been carefully prepared. He had learned all about the coming event. He knew that mother had just given birth and that now he had a beautiful baby brother. At last mother, baby, and the baby nurse came home from the hospital, and everyone was braced for trouble. But Robert surprised them all. He was quite calm and even showed moderate interest in the tiny infant. He stayed amiable for days, unruffled by the inevitable fuss surrounding the new arrival. Mother and father were delighted with this reaction and congratulated each other on having prepared him so well.

At the end of the week the baby nurse took her leave. With her suitcase packed, she said good-bye, gave Robert a farewell kiss, and started out the door. The little boy went racing after her. "Hey, lady," he called, "you forgot your baby!"

The arrival of a second child, as Robert abruptly discovered, is far from casual or temporary, but rather for everyone in the family an ongoing, rich, and very exciting experience. Also a complex one. A recent study of young parents from a wide range of backgrounds revealed that they found many long-term rewards in having a second child but, "universally, the parents felt that the immediate time after the birth of the second child was the hardest time of their marriage."

Certainly the arrival of baby number two is a peak event filled with much joy and satisfaction, but it also brings numerous demands and challenges—physical, economic, and emotional. As one psychologist has pointed out, the first baby is born to a couple, whereas the second baby is born to a family; and everything in the family constellation must shift and change to accommodate this new member.

In some ways the biggest impact, emotionally, involves the older sibling. Psychologist Alfred Adler refers to this event as the "de-throning" of the firstborn. For a little while, indeed, your first child was the tiny monarch of the family, on whom all interest and attention were happily focused. But the image is a bit exaggerated: It isn't so much that the first is dethroned, but rather that he or she must now share the throne with a sibling.

As we've already seen, the need to share parental concern and attention is a difficult concept for a young child to grasp. Young children think of love as a finite quantity. To a youngster's simple way of thinking, some of the love previously received will now be withdrawn and invested in another. Like a dish of ice cream or a glass of orange juice, if you give some to one, there's going to be less for the other. So it's a fact, and quite normal, that kids—especially younger ones—see the coming of a new baby as a threat to their position; to them the baby is a usurper and a disruption. Dr. Haim Ginott has noted that the coming of the second baby is a first-rate crisis in the life of a young child. But in time, given a warm, loving family environment, the older sibling usually does accept the new member and begins to enjoy the benefits of a sibling relationship. Even willful Robert will find his anxieties abating if his feelings and needs are treated with understanding: The real key to eventual acceptance of the baby is showing your firstborn that parental love and care will not be withdrawn and that it continues for all.

Basic guidelines to keep in mind are that your first child's life should be uprooted as little as possible, that the subject be dealt with simply but honestly, and that the youngster be firmly reassured as to his or her own secure, special place in the family group.

Preparing a child for a new baby involves both emotional and physical factors. Let's look at a few helpful approaches— first those concerning younger siblings, then those concerning children of school age.

PREPARING TODDLERS AND PRESCHOOLERS

Every child has the right to know ahead of time about the arrival of a newcomer. The surprising news has to be assimilated, thought about, adjusted to. But when should he or she be told? This will vary, depending on the child's age and general level of understanding. Remember that young children don't have a clear sense of the passage of time; the future is vague, and a month may seem like forever. A child told too soon will probably lose interest as the weeks and months go by. Or he or she may become bored with the whole idea and even forget. So it's best, where feasible, to hold off the announcement until the last few months of pregnancy.

Of course, a preschooler may ask questions about mother's changing shape or wonder why she's been getting tired or has to lie down often. If questions do come up, answering them provides a natural way to break the news. And it needn't be done with a lot of fanfare. It's enough to say, "We're going to have a baby in our family," or words to that effect. After that, you can play it by ear. If a youngster shows no more interest at this point, don't dwell on it.

If there is some interest and curiosity, which is often the case, talk about it further. Many children are fascinated with feeling mother's belly and learning a little more about the subject of birth. They may ask, "Was I in your tummy, too?" or "How does the baby know when to be born?" To which your answer can be, "When it's really ready. When it's just the right size." Remember in these discusions to keep answers simple, uncomplicated, truthful— and try not to tell too much all at once. This is big news for a two-, three-, or four-year-old, and it will take a bit of time to assimilate.

Let's look at some brief scenarios that indicate different ways the subject can be approached:

"Daddy and I love you so much, we think you're terrific, that we decided to have another baby *just like you.* Isn't that *wonderful?* You're going to *love* the new baby! The baby will love you, too. You'll be very proud of it. The two of you will play together all the time and have lots of fun!"

Obviously an explanation of this kind isn't honest and won't sound convincing to your child. By building up highly unrealistic expectations a parent is asking for trouble later on. Compare that approach with the following, which would of course take place over a period of time:

ADULT: We're going to have a baby in our family.
CHILD: When?
ADULT: Not for a while yet. In about two months—and that's a lot of days.
CHILD: Will it play with me?
ADULT: Sure—when the baby is big enough.
CHILD: I want a sister.
ADULT: Well, we won't know if it will be a sister or a brother until it's born. But Daddy and I will love either a sister *or* a brother. Just like we love you.

And later on:

CHILD: Where is the baby?
ADULT: Right here in Mommy's belly.
CHILD: I wanna see it. Can I see it?
ADULT: Not yet—but here, you can feel it.

You also might have:

CHILD: I don't want one. I don't want that baby.
ADULT: Sometimes boys and girls do feel like that. I know.
         That's okay. But Mommy and Daddy will still
         play with you and read to you, and take good care
         of you and love you.

As we've seen, these comments and discussions won't
come all at once. But over the passing days and weeks, talking to your child with candor and honesty is reassuring and
conveys the fact that you do grasp his or her feelings.

Naturally, as the birth draws nearer, it's awaited with
much anticipation. Parental feelings are usually mixed, involving excitement, impatience, anxiety, and so on. But for
your own sake as well as the child's, it's best to avoid extremes. The excitement should certainly be expressed and
shared, but try not to oversell the big event. New babies do
involve extra work, and for quite a while they won't be great
fun as young playmates. You can be frank about this. Talk to
your child about the baby's smallness and helplessness, the
fact that it will probably cry a lot, that it will need a good bit
of attention. It isn't fair to paint a glowing picture of endless
fun and games immediately in store for an older sibling. On
the other hand, you don't want to sound negative or apologize for the baby or suggest that a baby is nothing but a
headache. So, as always, when you talk of all this with your
youngster, try to strike a comfortable, commonsense balance.

Also, it isn't wise to promise specifically that a new baby will be either a boy or a girl—a prediction that can build false hopes and lead to disappointments. Nowadays, in certain special cases, amniocentesis is used to reveal the sex as well as the genetic makeup of the embryo; but these are atypical situations. So if your child announces, "I want a baby sister," or "I hope it's a boy," make sure he or she knows that you'll be delighted with the new baby whatever its gender.

Quite by chance one mother mentioned—within her four-year-old's hearing—that the doctor thought she might be carrying twins. The little boy was overjoyed at this unique prospect and couldn't wait to tell everyone he met. In due time he was presented with a fine, healthy baby brother, but the child felt very let down. "You," he said to the baby resentfully, "are supposed to be twins!" Another child, a little girl, yearned for a sister and convinced herself that the baby would be a girl. When she learned from her mother, who phoned from the hospital, that instead the baby was a boy, the child was very unhappy. "Isn't there somebody at the hospital," she asked, "who you can trade with?"

Such minor disappointments wear off fairly quickly, but they do highlight the pitfalls of allowing youngsters to build up high expectations.

In general, there are three points to keep in mind when telling your firstborn about the impending birth:

- Be frank, not secretive. Answer your child's questions honestly and simply, with tact and loving common sense.
- Watch your "data input." Respond warmly to your child's interest, by all means, but don't overload the youngster with more details than he or she really wants or can handle.
- Share with your preschooler your joyful expectations, but don't gush or grow overenthusiastic. It's unwise to paint an over-idealized, roseate picture that may lead to disillusionment.

Preparing for the new baby has a practical as well as emotional side. There will be baby clothes and other things to buy; living arrangements at home may have to be changed; and so on.

Here again, it helps to let your older child participate in these activities—if he or she shows any interest in doing so. Some preschoolers enjoy going with mother on brief shopping trips for things the baby will need. Some enjoy helping to arrange furniture in baby's room. If the room is to be shared with the older child, he or she should be included in the planning. In short, everything should and can be done to make the older child feel like a participant in these arrangements. But in the excitement, don't neglect the deeper feelings. It's vital that your child not be given the impression that she or he is being shunted aside, that his crib or high chair is simply being snatched away and awarded to another. Make sure your child understands that a place is being made for the new baby—but *not* at the expense of his own needs.

Is your child about four years of age? If so, this may be an excellent time to present her or him with a real "grown-up" bed, freeing the crib for baby's use. If you do so, try to provide the bed early enough in the pregnancy so that it won't be viewed as a deprivation of the crib. Then later, the crib might be repainted, with your child helping. This can be an exciting event for a preschooler, an event that makes the child truly feel older and that compensates for other disruptive changes.

It all adds up to a simple goal: By sharing preparations, within reason, the firstborn can come to regard the new baby not merely as Mommy's and Daddy's, but as the family's baby. On a deeper level, taking part in these arrangements helps to soften a child's sense of being passively acted upon, or "done to."

The Separation Period

Although there's a trend toward giving birth at home, most women still go to a hospital or birthing center to have their babies. In previous years mothers stayed in the hospital for about two weeks, which often created a problem as to what to do about older children in the family. Today, hospital stays are much shorter. In addition many fathers now obtain special leaves from their work, so the separation period may be far less disruptive.

If father isn't available to look after the older child, arrangements can be made for a grandparent, other relative, or trusted friend whom the child knows well, to move in for a few days. In any event, it's best to continue young children in their regular, accustomed routines at home.

Also, make sure beforehand that your child knows you'll be going to the hospital. Reassure the youngster that it will only be for a few days and that when you come home, you'll have the baby with you. Toward the very end of the pregnancy, you can mention to the child that you may have to go to the hospital at night. It's traumatic for a toddler or preschooler to wake up in the morning and find Mommy gone, so a little forewarning is a good idea. You might also let your youngster help you pack the small suitcase you'll be taking. If the child asks questions or expresses anxiety, by all means explain that although giving birth isn't dangerous, it's easier for a mother to be in a hospital, where the doctor can help.

What about hospital visits? Recent studies show that there are benefits in allowing an older child to visit Mother during her stay and to see the baby either in her hospital room or in the nursery. If there is a rooming-in arrangement, such a visit might be possible. However, most hospitals—because of fears of infection and generally entrenched practices—have rules against this. If visits aren't feasible, of course there's always the telephone, and regular phone calls to your little one are highly recommended. Mother might also leave a special gift behind, a stuffed toy or doll, a little token reminder for your youngster during this short separation.

Sometimes, when Mother first comes home, a toddler or preschooler may show resentment at her "desertion"—turning away from her, rejecting kisses, and so on. But this is usually short-lived, and the child quickly gets over it, especially when given a little extra attention and love.

While a visit by your firstborn to the maternity ward can be beneficial, it isn't always possible, nor is it really essential. In general, children do manage quite well at home without hospital contacts. According to the findings of the Gesell Institute of Human Development,

> With the hospital stay currently so short, many experts feel that any visiting by the child at the hospital might best be omitted, and that the introduction to the new baby is best accomplished in the safety of the child's own home.

Bringing Baby Home
The moment when you and baby come back from the hospital is bound to be a happy, exciting event for the whole family. Some people feel that this particular moment can be smoother and easier if the older child isn't present, but most authorities say otherwise. Remember that this is the *family's* baby—your older child has the right to be there and to take part in the big event. On the other hand, an older sib will have natural apprehension about this new arrival. For all your assurance and loving attention, the youngster is bound to be anxious about the "intruder." So common sense says to temper your excitement a bit: Don't overplay baby's arrival. Conversely, don't underplay it by acting too casual. The point to make is that you're home at last, the family is together, and you're very happy to see your older child again.

One good way to share this homecoming is to let the sibling make the phone calls to announce the news. Your child is given the task (with your help) of phoning grandparents, other relatives, and friends to tell them that "Mommy and the baby are home," which for a youngster is an exciting and involving role.

Unless your firstborn specifically rejects the idea and ignores the newcomer, let him or her get to know the infant right from the start. Let the child touch the baby, help to unwrap it, and hold it—with supervision, of course. Even toddlers can be included in the bathing of the baby or in rocking it to sleep. If you're bottle-feeding baby, let the older child help get the bottle ready. Better still (and this works for boys as well as girls), your little one may want to model the whole process using a doll and toy bottle. For a two-, three-, or four-year-old, imitating with a baby doll—feeding, changing, dressing it, and so on—can be a very positive activity at this particular time.

If your breast-feeding your baby, do so naturally, without excluding the other child. Some children, seeing the special closeness and intimacy of Mommy nursing baby, may be upset, especially toddlers. But most experts do advise being open and casual. This is something the toddler can and will get used to, and your aim is to keep family patterns normal and natural.

Once again, keep in mind that the needs of your firstborn are as valid as the needs of your baby. Of course you'll be hard-pressed, in those first months, to take care of baby and also pay enough attention to your older child, but it can be done and is well worth the effort. Baby's needs are vital, but your time still has to be shared. So don't put off an older child's reasonable demands. Try to watch remarks like, "Tell me about it later," or "Can't you see I'm busy with the baby?" If your replies signal to the child that he is being neglected because of the baby, it only reinforces the budding feelings of sibling rivalry. So try not to link an older child's needs with baby's needs.

Don't let your firstborn's regular interests and friendships get sidetracked. Where possible, tend to baby when the older one is in nursery school or otherwise occupied. And re-member—the quality of your attention is what counts most. Arrange to spend private time with the older child as often as feasible. Take him or her places without the baby; and when you and your firstborn are together, make sure that your attention is fully focused on that child alone.

Some modern parents, aware of the potential for jealousy, bend over backward in an attempt to avoid it. They virtually "ignore" the new baby in a zealous effort to spare the feelings of their firstborn. But this is both unrealistic and unwise. Unrealistic, because it skirts a natural rivalry problem that should be met and dealt with honestly. Unwise, because it conveys a false picture of family life to the sibling; it delivers a distorted message to him or her about how small babies are treated by parents. Again, sheltering your firstborn too thoroughly from facing the fact of a new baby in the house does the child a disservice and can lead to complications later.

Finally, let's remember that the reactions of a young child aren't always predictable. All the aforementioned suggestions have to be adapted to fit your own situation. Some toddlers and preschoolers respond with great delight to the arrival of a baby. Some can be openly hostile. Others may seem, on the surface, fairly indifferent. But the principle still applies: Regardless of stresses, strains, and extra demands on parents, the aim is to keep an older child from feeling neglected and pushed aside, to reassure him or her that indeed there's enough parental love and consideration to go around. Your first child does need help in adapting to the newcomer's presence and accepting baby's legitimate place in the family circle. A big order, yes—but tact, consideration, and a loving approach can make it all work.

When Visitors Come
In the wake of your new baby, you're sure to have a tide of visitors; proud grandparents, aunts, uncles, and friends will all be anxious to see the infant and to bring gifts.

For the older child this is a difficult time, since it again puts baby very much in the spotlight. But there are many little ways to ease the situation. People who come to visit can be quietly encouraged to pay some attention to the other child, or children, as well. Sometimes the child can be delegated to show the new baby to the guests. Some of these visitors may thoughtfully bring a small present for the older child. If not, it's a good idea to provide some yourself. One young mother kept a box of small trifles in the hall closet; when guests arrived, she supplied them with something earmarked for the older sibling. As a result, the child greeted visitors with much eagerness.

It also helps to remind your older ones that when they were babies, they too were showered with gifts and attentions and that everyone made a big fuss over them.

Some of the visiting, conversation, inevitable oohing and ahhing will take place without the older child present. But if your child is on hand, and the conversation seems to be exclusively about the baby, you can subtly bring your older child into it. Ask the child to show your guests his or her latest drawing or nursery school project. Mention how helpful he or she has been in assisting with the baby. In short, acknowledge your sibling as an individual with much to offer. All it takes is a comment such as "Sally's been so helpful with the baby. It made things a lot easier for us." Or, "You can't imagine how well Bobby managed while I was away. He's been terrific."

One kind of well-wishing that enthusiastic visitors sometimes indulge in relates to sex stereotyping: "Aren't you lucky to have a boy this time! Now Ed will have someone to go to ball games with!" Such remarks in the presence of an older girl can only worsen a relationship that's already fraught with feelings of rejection. Parents can't always regulate the conversation of visitors, but they can watch for this kind of stereotyping and ease its impact on a sibling. To the remark, "Aren't you lucky to have a boy this time!" a sensitive parent can reply, "We've been lucky twice—first to have a girl and now to have a boy!" And it's important that the reply be made immediately, not at a later time after the visitors have gone. The older sibling needs to see the parent as a partisan, and she needs it when the "offense" is committed.

We're also familiar with the kind of old-fashioned stereotyping that still at times occurs with the arrival of a male. For many generations male babies were looked on as a particular blessing, an echo from earlier societies in which the birth of a boy, for sheer economic reasons, was more desirable and practical than the birth of a female. Even though (at least in modern, affluent societies) such reasons have long disappeared, the old tradition persists.

To a lesser degree sex-stereotyped remarks can work the other way, too, as may happen for example if a girl baby is born after a number of males. Here the reaction is often, "Aren't you lucky! A darling little girl, after so many boys!" For any boys who might be listening, the implication is that this female child is much more lovable and will be much more rewarding to the parents.

Dealing with visitors and well-wishers may seem a fairly small matter, but even the youngest children have well-developed antennae that pick up unintentional put-downs. Parents need to keep their own ears tuned so that they can make these occasions a genuine family celebration.

JEALOUSY AND REGRESSION

"We don't need a baby here."
"Let's give him away."
"I hate that dumb baby!"
"Why don't you take her back to the hospital?"

Sometimes toddlers and preschoolers express their jealousy with frank and blunt comments. Sometimes the anger and resentment are hidden and will surface more subtly. Sibling feelings are complex and elusive; they may appear in any number of ways and over a long period of time. But we can be sure of one thing: A degree of jealousy and rivalry is a fact of sibling life—it's there and it's natural.

No matter how well a young child is prepared, no matter how carefully parents consider needs and feelings, the toddler's cozy, self-centered world has now been drastically changed. "Jealousy, envy, and rivalry will inevitably be there," writes child psychologist, Dr. Haim Ginott. "To fail to anticipate them, or to be shocked at their appearance, is an ignorance that is far from bliss."

To a toddler the coming of a baby is simply (in his or her eyes) a security threat, and just as with adults, a threat of this sort can't help but arouse strong feelings. When a youngster acts up over the baby and causes difficulties, the child is really attempting to defend his or her emotional turf. In simple, crude ways, the sibling lashes out at circumstance. But these negative reactions can be eased, and some perhaps eliminated, by the wisdom and skill with which parents approach the subject.

Overt Behavior

Envy may not appear right away when you first bring baby home. The excitement of the moment, the fact that Mother is back again, are big distractions to a young child. Later, when the family settles into new routines, the toddler will grow more aware of his or her change in status. Sometimes it isn't until the baby is mobile—able to actively interfere with the older child's play—that strong resentments will appear. But this may happen earlier, after six or seven months, when baby begins to take on the aspect of a real person instead of a passive, helpless doll. With this emergence of baby's own personality, the sibling may start to feel threatened.

We know that some of the toddler's anger is really directed at the parents for bringing home a "replacement." But of course it's safer for a child to show hostility toward a tiny infant than toward big, all-powerful Mommy and Daddy. With baby as the target, jealousy can be expressed in physical assaults—hugging the infant too hard, squeezing, pinching, biting, pulling, even punching it. One mother was overheard saying, "Billy really adores his little brother; he hugs him and hugs him so tightly that the baby starts to cry."

Remember that little children haven't got our built-in behavior safeguards, and these physical assaults can sometimes be dangerous. So it's a wise idea to keep a close eye on your toddler for a while, to see what the reactions will be. The psychologists at the Gesell Institute advise parents not to leave an infant alone in the room for very long with a sibling who's less than six or seven years old. The institute acknowledges that this may sound extreme, but it prefers to be over-cautious in protecting babies.

Certainly not all toddlers or preschoolers behave violently and aggressively, but care should be taken. The clear rule must be that there will be no hurting of the baby, at any time. This should be emphasized as firmly as possible. "Babies can be easily hurt, so we want to be very careful," is a good guideline for your child, whether there's been trouble or not. And, "There will be no hitting or hurting the baby in this family," is a simple rule that all youngsters can understand.

In addition to rules, parents can offer other alternatives to young siblings. With a toddler who seems particularly aggressive, you might try giving him or her a large stuffed toy or doll on which the child can then vent hostility. In this acting-out process, the youngster can spank the doll, punch it, throw it on the floor, jump on it, and so on. With care a parent can initiate this process, but then should stand by as a neutral observer, making no judgments, accepting the harmless drama in which the sibling airs his or her honest feelings on an inanimate object (instead of on baby or self).

During this ritual, parental comments can be brief and straightforward:

"Now I can see how angry you are."
"You really are mad at the baby."
"I know you're angry—I can see that."

Finally the child is reminded that there must be *no* hitting of the baby and also told, "Whenever you feel really angry, you can come and show me, like this." Many psychologists believe that this type of safe ventilation is more effective than simply threatening the child with punishment or scolding the toddler for being "cruel and thoughtless" toward an infant.

Besides *acting out*, there is the very effective and less controversial process of *talking out*. This is more suitable for preschoolers, even school-aged children—but should be used sparingly, in moderation. Parents have to be careful not to assume the role of professional psychologist in dealing with sibling feelings, but vocalizing is now looked on as effective therapy, if the child is old enough to participate.

In this process, frank words are substituted for harmful behavior, and the child is able to voice deep, often scary thoughts without fear and without guilt. If your young one gets very sulky whenever you feed the baby, for example, you might say,

> "When I'm feeding the baby and taking care of it, I think you may feel a little left out. Maybe you're kind of jealous, right? Or you think we don't love you. Well, *whenever* you feel that way, when you're jealous or angry, come and tell me. Be *sure* to tell me, okay? Talk about it to me or to Daddy. We'll listen, and we'll give you lots of extra love."

In bringing up the subject of jealousy, you won't be telling a child anything new—but what you will do is signal that these feelings are okay, that you understand them, and that you'll help your child cope with them. Encouraging a child to talk it out does away with hidden guilt and invites a free flow of trust and communication that can become a wonderful pattern for the child's later years. As we have already pointed out, the child is bound to feel some degree of hurt, anger, resentment, or rejection. It's much better to help children voice these feelings than to have them suppressed in silence.

Repressed feelings, even in the very young, can grow and fester. One mother, who made a point of verbalizing these matters with her child, said,

> At first I was shocked, you know. I mean really upset. I didn't like hearing Petey say he hated the baby and things like that. But we kept talking, and I reassured him, and after a while it gave me a kind of freedom. Like a door opening. Petey feels it, too. Now, when he's upset about the baby, or anything,

he comes and tells me about it. It helps him a lot—and I think it's brought us closer to each other.

Buried Feelings

- Three-and-a-half-year-old Gina was good as gold when her mother came home with the new baby. She showed only mild interest in her little brother. In general she was docile and passive and didn't react strongly to the baby one way or the other. Her parents weren't greatly surprised, since Gina had always been a rather quiet child. But after a few weeks, Gina began having nightmares. She would wake up screaming with fear, then would run into the baby's room to see if he was all right.
- Andy, four years old, was pleased when his baby sister was born. His parents encouraged this attitude; they constantly reminded him how much he truly loved his new sister and how happy everyone was with this new addition to the family. Soon Andy began to wake up at night, wheezing and gasping. He developed a case of asthma, but the doctor couldn't seem to find any physical basis for Andy's recurring attacks.

It's no secret that feelings can be suppressed but that they rarely disappear. One way or another they'll eventually surface, usually in destructive forms. In Gina's case, her parents—through tactful, probing questions—learned that in her nightmares she dreamed that she kept pushing her baby brother out the window. Waking up terrified, she would rush into his room to make sure it wasn't true. With help from her parents, Gina was gradually able to talk about her hostile feelings. She was reassured by them that it was okay to be angry at the baby and to feel jealous. Putting thoughts into actual words—words that were accepted by Mommy and Daddy—helped to ease Gina's anxieties, and the nightmares finally stopped.

In Andy's case, because the doctor couldn't find an allergic or other physical basis of the asthma, his parents went to a child psychologist for help. After a few sessions with Andy, it became apparent that the boy was feeling great pressure at home to "love, love, love" his baby sister. Guilty about his covered-up resentments, the problem literally took the form of physical pressure on his chest. Again, by getting Andy to talk of his real feelings—and having his parents acknowledge and accept them—the child's breathing attacks diminished. Eventually they disappeared.

Every case history doesn't apply to every child—siblings don't all react to a new baby with nightmares or asthma— but such examples give us insights: Suppressing natural feelings can indeed lead to harmful symptoms and actions. And if a child can't, or is afraid to, express these feelings safely, they will usually surface in other ways. Some young siblings become aimlessly destructive, breaking plates or smashing once-loved toys. Some may develop skin rashes. Others bite their nails or begin to pull their hair (safer, of course, than pulling the baby's hair). Many of these symptoms will dissipate with the passage of time, but parents can help to ease their toddlers' paths by helping youngsters to unlock natural feelings that, in former years, were considered shocking and improper. And of course where symptoms persist, the help of a child psychologist may be required.

"I'm a Baby, Too!"

Another reaction, familiar to many parents, is for a toddler or preschooler to regress into the actions of his or her own babyhood. The child may forget toilet training and begin to soil again or wet the bed. He or she may demand a bottle once more, begin to crawl, suck a thumb, or try to climb into the crib with the baby. The child may also have crying fits or temper tantrums.

These regressions serve a double purpose. In one sense they're a young child's attempt to draw parental attention away from the baby, by behaving disruptively: "If I do in my pants, Mommy will have to leave the baby alone and take care of me."

Secondly, the child may make a bid for attention and love by trying to actually become a baby once more: "Mommy is always fussing with that baby, so I'll be a baby, too."

These backslidings are relatively harmless and commonplace, and can be allowed, within reason. Also, when treated by parents with patience and sensitivity, they tend to disappear within a short period. It's good to remember that growth in children is a jagged process—two steps forward, then back a step, or sometimes back two steps! Whatever the retrogression, don't shame or humiliate your child for acting babyish: "Stop acting like a baby; you're a big girl now," is perhaps the worst thing you can say to a child in such a situation. Once the older child adjusts to the infant intruder—and finds that he or she has not in fact been cast aside—the need to be a baby again diminishes. But these symptoms are rather touching. They point out to us again how desperately our little ones need constant adult support and affection.

Children who do regress can be helped in various little ways. Parents can point out to them the great advantages of being two, three, or four years old, as compared with being a small passive infant who can't run and play and have fun. In addition, the child should be highly praised for his or her grown-up behavior—the fact that the child can dress himself or herself, help clean up a room, tidy up in the kitchen, and so on. These and similar reinforcements remind a young sibling of the real joy and excitement of growing and learning.

Again, we must remember that sibling jealousy can't be totally prevented—but it can be tempered. By encouraging and supporting children in their emerging activities and interests, by showing acceptance and sympathy for their moments of stress and envy, we ease the transitions and smooth out many of the emotional bumps.

PREPARING THE SCHOOL-AGE CHILD

Warren S., now in his thirties, recalls how he felt when his younger sister was born:

I was seven years old when Mother came home from the hospital with my baby sister, Julie. I remember it quite clearly because my parents, aunts, and uncles had all prepared me well. It was a big event of course, and everyone made a fuss over the baby. But it didn't particularly get to me. I was curious, sure, but it didn't seem too important. At that point I was in school, I was learning to read and to draw. And to use my new roller skates. We city kids all started on roller skates early! The fact is, *my* life was very exciting. Lots was happening, you know? And a baby sister didn't really affect me that much. Later, when Julie was six or seven, I remember there was some competition and rivalry. We had our fights and squabbles, but it wasn't a big thing. The age gap, and the sex gap, kind of distanced us. Now that we're adults, we get along very well. I like to play "big brother" and I feel protective toward her. We share our problems now and appreciate having each other to talk to and lean on.

Studies show that the greater the age gap between siblings, the less envy tends to be present. The greatest stress occurs where the first child is three or four years old or younger, at the time the second baby arrives. Where an older child is five, there are fewer tensions. And with a first child who is six, seven, eight, or more, there's often less friction.

School-age kids growing up in a healthy environment have a fairly strong sense of self. They've begun to develop friends and interests away from home. Since they feel less dependent on Mother and Father, they feel more in control of their own lives. As a result, a new baby will be seen not as a dire threat but simply as an interesting, novel, and sometimes annoying addition to the family circle.

A child of eight or nine may take a genuine interest in the new sibling and want to participate in its care. Most school-age children do get a sense of enjoyment out of doing little things for a baby. They will baby-sit, help with feedings, run small errands. They especially like to play with the baby and will spend a lot of time talking and singing to it, also teaching it simple words and games. Almost all kids in these "middle" years like to play teacher—and a baby sibling gives them a wonderful chance to act out this grown-up role.

But we have to keep in mind that school-age sibs are still children themselves. While they often behave calmly and responsibly, there will be jealousy too. A new baby is, after all, a disruption; family patterns and living space have to be changed, schedules rearranged, and time formerly spent with the older one must now be allocated to baby. So infants may have to be protected from the unthinking or careless behavior of older children.

Conversely, when baby begins to crawl and walk, the *older* child may need protection from interference by the toddler. Joan J., a Los Angeles mother of two, recalls,

> Beth, my three-year-old, got along fine with her baby brother when he was in the crib, then just learning to crawl. She loved to hold his hands and help him take his first tiny steps. But later, when he became a full-fledged toddler— forget it! Ricky was like a tornado, going everywhere, getting into everything. He interfered a lot with Beth and her friends and their games. If they were playing jacks, for instance, or building with blocks, he'd barge right in and wreck it. *He* didn't need protection, but *she* did—and I had to keep my eyes open to see she wasn't driven crazy. Fortunately Beth was good-natured about it, but it really was a tough time for her.

Studies also show that where there are *two* older siblings, the middle child feels more of the rivalry, while the oldest child feels more of the pleasure. Often the oldest may become quite fatherly or motherly toward the baby, while the younger sibling may turn whiny and revert to babyish ways. The reason is fairly simple: The oldest child has already been through the trauma of displacement by the arrival of a baby and has more or less made peace with the idea. For the second child, however, the coming of a baby is a brand-new, jarring experience. Instead of being the youngest, with its special privileges, this position has now been usurped. And being caught in the middle can be a tough role for any child to adjust to.

What this tells us is that even school-age kids need time to absorb and accept a new family member. But the same guidelines apply as those for toddlers and preschoolers. With parental consideration, sympathy, and respect, older kids generally make the transition very successfully and will often, in time, find the new baby an enjoyable element in their young lives.

HELPFUL BOOKS

For toddlers (older children as well) many fine books are available dealing with sibling relationships. Charming and well illustrated, these stories are aimed directly at siblings of various ages and cover many of the questions that may arise both before and after the arrival of a new baby.

It's an excellent idea—particularly if you're preparing a firstborn for the big event—to obtain some of this literature. Read the books to your young one; if the child is old enough, encourage him or her to do the reading. It's a rare child who doesn't love to have a parent read to him, and toddlers especially like a bedtime story-reading session. This may be an excellent time to introduce one of the better picture books, such as *When the New Baby Comes, I'm Moving Out* by Martha Alexander, which will help to prepare a youngster for the arrival of an infant. Books are, of course, one safe step removed from reality, and therefore easier for a child to cope with. They not only give youngsters insight and information, but allow a chance to verbalize personal doubts and fears. Books, tapes, and records also give children other figures in this same situation with whom they can identify because they share their feelings and concerns.

Here is a list of recommended books, with brief content descriptions, which can be of help in this area:

Peter's Chair by Ezra Jack Keats (Harper & Row).

First they paint Peter's old cradle pink for the new baby. Then they paint his crib pink. He decides to rescue his one remaining baby chair and run away. Outside on the street, he tries to rest on the little chair and finds he's much too big to fit. Peter's rebellion ends when he returns home and suggests that they paint the little chair pink also.

That New Baby! by Patricia Relf (Golden Press).

In this bright picture book, three-year-old Elizabeth discovers what it's like to have a baby brother. Her jealousy begins when he is brought home from the hospital, but as Mikey grows and begins to walk and talk, Elizabeth finds there are satisfactions in being a big sister.

She Come Bringing Me That Little Baby Girl by Eloise Greenfield (J. B. Lippincott).

A familiar story of jealousy with a new twist: Kevin's disappointment that the baby is a girl is alleviated when mother points out that *she* was a baby girl once and that her big brother (the uncle whom Kevin loves) took good care of her. This new perspective helps Kevin feel more accepting toward the newcomer.

Lucky Stiff! by Gen LeRoy (McGraw-Hill).

School-age Anabel resents it and feels left out when baby brother arrives. Because of the attention he receives, she calls him a "lucky stiff." Later, playing house with her friends, she takes the role of baby. Lying there in her makeshift "crib" while her friends romp and play, Anabel decides that maybe being a passive little infant isn't much fun after all.

The One in the Middle Is the Green Kangaroo by Judy Blume (Bradbury Press).

Freddy, the sibling in the middle, feels like "the peanut butter part of a sandwich," squeezed between his older brother and his baby sister. His self-image is redeemed when he gets to play a very special part in the school play—because his size is just right.

We Are Having a Baby by Viki Holland (Scribner's).

Four-year-old Dana, confused and unhappy over the arrival of her new baby brother, is helped by kind, loving, understanding parents. A simple story told beautifully through sensitive photographs.

My Brother Fine with Me by Lucille Clifton (Holt, Rinehart).
A young boy is considered a nuisance by his older sister
until he runs away. This startles her and gives her a different viewpoint. Told in Black English, with appealing
pictures.

Nobody Asked Me If I Wanted a Baby Sister by Martha Alexander (Dial Press).
A young boy, resentful of his baby sister, plans to give her
away. But he discovers that when baby cries, he's one of
the few people who can comfort and console her. This
helps him change his mind; he decides the family should
keep her after all.

When the New Baby Comes, I'm Moving Out by Martha Alexander (Dial Press).
A companion book to the preceding one. Oliver is very
annoyed at mother's preparations for the baby, due soon.
He fantasizes getting rid of mother and running away. In
the end, she finds a way to persuade him of his importance
to her and the family.

Sometimes I'm Jealous by Jane Werner Watson (Golden Press).
A three-page introduction explains to parents a child's feelings when a new baby comes. Then, in a simple first-
person narrative, a child talks out the whole story of these
feelings, from the time he is the center of attention, to his
displacement, and finally to acceptance of the situation.

Stevie by John Steptoe (Harper & Row).
Robert is an only child. A younger boy, Stevie, comes to
stay with them temporarily and assumes the role of Robert's sibling. Robert looks on Stevie as a big, fat annoyance—but when the boy leaves at last, Robert feels
lonely. He finds that he really misses little Stevie.

Hugging, Hitting and Other Family Matters by Naomi Hample
(Dial Press).
Josh writes, "The thing I like best about my family is that
whenever there is a fight we always make up after." In this
unique book, some seventy children (first- to seventh-
graders) put down in their own handwriting their ideas

and feelings: why we need families, what's good (or bad) about having brothers and sisters, and so on.

Fanny's Sister by Penelope Lively (Dutton).
Fanny is upset when another child is born into the family. She makes a very mean wish, which she regrets when it almost (but not quite) seems to be coming true.

Betsy's Baby Brother by Gunilla Wolde (Random House).
A small, charming picture book, detailing Betsy's reactions to her baby brother. Here the jealousy is minimized, and more attention is paid to how Betsy helps her mother take care of the new infant. Particularly useful because of its upbeat approach.

TIPS AND SUGGESTIONS

Here are a few capsule suggestions that may be of help, based on material in the preceding pages:

- Do inform your toddler or preschooler that a new baby is coming—*but* don't overload the child with too much information too soon. Try to space the news out in a natural, simple way; and answer questions truthfully.
- Do share with your youngster the pleasure and anticipation of the coming birth—*but* don't paint a rosy, unrealistic picture of all this, which may lead to disillusionment later.
- Do encourage your young child to help with physical arrangements for the baby—*but* don't give the impression that the sibling's own needs are being ignored during these changes.
- Do let your firstborn join in the excitement of baby's homecoming—*but* don't overplay the arrival of the newcomer. Conversely, don't act casual or indifferent about it, which would be less than honest.
- Do let your young child participate in caring for baby with simple, easily managed chores—*but* don't press this matter if there's no interest on the youngster's part.
- Do remember that, at this crucial time, your firstborn

needs your attention and understanding more than ever—*but* don't lean over backward to the point of hiding or neglecting attention to your baby's needs.

· Do enforce a firm rule that there must be "no hitting or hurting the baby"—*but* don't deny your firstborn the right to verbalize his or her natural feelings. A certain amount of "talking out" can help to ease many pressures.

· Do be prepared for a possible return to babyish ways by your toddler or preschooler—*but* don't react excessively to this. With a little time, plus sympathy and patience on your part, the child's regressive behavior will disappear.

· Do encourage your older, school-age youngsters to be helpful with the new baby—*but* don't forget that older sibs are children too and still need a great deal of guidance, love, and parental understanding.

· Do make use of the excellent books now available to young siblings—*but* don't expect books to do it all. You and your spouse, as parents, bear the main responsibility in helping your youngsters to deal with their natural anxieties and conflicting feelings.

CHAPTER
7

Parents Talk about the Second Baby

The arrival of baby number two is, as we've seen, a major disruption in the neat, self-centered world of the firstborn. But the older child's reactions may vary greatly, just as the personalities of children vary. The response is sometimes immediate; in other cases it takes a while to become apparent. In some families a firstborn's real feelings may be deeply buried, only to erupt later in destructive behavior that seems quite removed from the arrival of the new infant. And at times sibling hostility seems aimed not at the baby at all, but at mother, the villain in the scenario.

The following comments by parents offer some idea of the nature of these reactions—and point up various ways of dealing with them.

Sally T., mother of David, age ten, and Libby, age thirteen: "Both of my kids are past the baby stage and get along fairly well, but it wasn't that way in the beginning. Now I find it kind of painful to go back to those days. Back to the sibling rivalry. It also reminds me of something I've always regretted—the fact that I wasn't aware of what a poor sense of time children have. Libby was three years and three months when I went to the hospital to have Davey—and I'm sorry that I didn't make her a calendar, a little four-day calendar so she could keep track of the time.

"Back then, I wasn't working. I was home all the time and I'd raised Libby without outside help, and she and I were incredibly close. We'd sort of had a 'honeymoon' that lasted three years, and we hardly ever had a fight. Then I went to the hospital to have this new baby, and it was this separation that really got to her. . . .

"Of course we'd prepared her for the baby in all kinds of ways. We only told her in the last month or two, I'm not exactly sure when. But we did know enough about her to realize she couldn't sit there for seven months waiting and waiting. So we told her toward the end, and that was fine. She hadn't really noticed anything except that I was nauseous for a couple of months—but she didn't connect it in any way with a baby. Certainly by the time I was six weeks away from being due, she did know about it and looked forward to it. The day before David came, she knew that her friend's mother would pick her up, that Daddy would be at the hospital, and that after the baby was born, Daddy would come home and be with her.

"There were no problems in our arrangements at home. Sometime before Davey was due, Bob and I moved to a bigger apartment. So instead of having a little room behind the kitchen, Libby had this big new room full of light—and then David's room was going to be the one behind the kitchen. She still had her crib, and she said, 'You know, some people give their child's own crib to their new baby. Isn't that *terrible*?' I said, 'Well, don't worry. You'll have your crib as long as you want it.' You know, we were supposedly doing everything right—that's what kills me. And then, the day before he was born, she said, 'Now remember, I want one of those sisters . . . that's the kind with the penis, isn't it?' I said, 'No, honey, the kind with the penis is a brother.' 'Oh, a brother!' she said. 'I want a brother.' So I said well, we couldn't tell and all that; it was something we couldn't choose, but it didn't really matter. Daddy and I would love either one. And then I went off to the hospital.

"Thinking back, I just feel, I just wish she'd had her calendar. Now this may be an illusion. All parents think, 'If only' . . . 'If only I hadn't taken the blanket away' . . . 'If only I'd done this or that.' . . . But I wish I'd made a chart with the days so Libby could check them off—one, two, three, and on the fourth we'd see each other again. A small point, but I do think it was really traumatic for her. Nothing awful happened. But when I got home, she wouldn't come near me; she stayed away, and she was *very* angry-looking! She kind of stood me off. I bent down next to her, so glad to see her. She looked so enormous to me, 'cause I'd been spending all my time with this tiny seven-pound baby! I remember bending down in front of her, and she stood there looking very furious and kind of sealed up inside of herself. And finally she said, 'Well, is it here?' And I said, 'Yes. He's here. He's asleep.' And she said, 'Can I see it?' I said yes and I took her down the hall. David was half-asleep in his crib, and I showed him to her, and her face suddenly broke open in this look of joy and amazement. She was *very* excited and she had three questions, right in a row: 'Can I hold him? Can I see his penis? Is he really mine?'

"And I said, 'Yes, you can hold him.' So I sat her right down, picked him up, and put him right in her arms there on the floor. For the moment she forgot all about being mad at me; it was lovely. I said, 'Later, when I change him, you can see the rest of him.' Then I said, 'He's really your brother. He belongs to himself the way you belong to yourself—but he's really your brother.'

"Well, they got along beautifully for about nine months. She'd fuss over him and get upset if he cried, even at the first peep. David adored her; she was the first one he smiled at, and he smiled whenever she was around. We were very encouraged, told her what a big help she was, and all that, and we tried to tone down the fuss over the baby, especially when Libby's grandparents came. But after about nine or ten months, when David was doing a lot of crawling around, it changed.

"At that point I think he crawled over to a big blockcastle Libby had just built and knocked it over. And for about a year and a half or two years we entered a state of what I called 'total war.' Oh yes, they played together, and we have photos of them kissing—but that was also the only period when I ever spanked her hard, when she'd go after him with the intent to really *hurt* him. I remember that happened maybe three or four times. Oh, that was an awful period. Also, what I remember doing during that period—I thought it was right then and I still do—though a lot of my friends thought it was wrong. What we did was, when she wasn't within his hearing, she could say to Bob or to me, 'I hate him! I wish he would die. I want him to go right out the window!' And I would answer, 'Yes, I know you do. That's pretty clear.'

"Bob and I would say to Libby over and over, 'You can think anything you want to think, and you can say to *us* anything you want to say, but you can't hurt him. We won't let you hurt him. People just can't do that to each other. It's wrong.'

"We had definite rules, and she knew it; she knew we'd be furious if she tried to hurt him. But she was able to let it all out verbally. Now I'll come to the end of this story a little early: I really don't know today of any brother and sister whose relationship is better than theirs is. They really do get on well, and they have for about four or five years—slowly getting to that point.

"After the period of 'total war' there was a period of 'medium war.' Still plenty of rivalry, believe me; but their relationship gradually changed. For instance Libby discovered that, as Davey got older, she had this great talent for amusing and entertaining him. She really latched onto this 'social skill' I guess you'd call it. She was very shy in those days, but with David she was just a dazzling star. No shyness at all! Of course they still flare up at each other, but he's not passive with her anymore; he can very well hold his own. And they really enjoy having little private conversations, with a lot of jokes and laughter. Humor seems to be the way they diffuse their competition. . . .

"Looking back, the most important thing to me was, I think, the business of letting her say what she felt. I just can't emphasize that enough. I feel a kind of triumphant sense now, because we were really going against the advice of a lot of people who thought we'd just be encouraging the hostility. But I feel it worked out fine. When the second baby comes, you think it's going to be pure joy, and it is—but there's also a lot of work and problems, and most of the time you're totally exhausted. There's joy certainly, but it was a big push in the beginning, managing two little ones. Still, I think Bob and I would do it again in pretty much the same way. . . ."

Laurel O., mother of Valerie, age five; Peter, age nine; and Christopher, age twelve: "Chris, our first boy, was three years and one month old when the second baby came along. We were so delighted with Chris and were enjoying him so much, we felt ready for another. Also Chris kept talking about having a baby brother, really longing for one—at least that's what he said. . . .

"I don't remember exactly when we told him he was going to have a brother or a sister. It just happened naturally—but we did tell him too early, which was a mistake, because the months stretched out, and he couldn't grasp that kind of time span. I recall there were repeated questions, many questions about how babies were born. I remember being amazed at the number of times that I'd be giving the same answers to the same questions, then being asked again by the same child, and having to repeat it all. I don't know why that came as such a surprise to me, because most things do need to be repeated to children, and this was such an abstract thing. They really can't understand it just from words.

"Well, when I came home from the hospital, the enthusiasm was still there. At that time Chris had a doll that he occasionally played with. When the baby turned out to be a boy, Chris decided his doll was a boy, too. He continued for a while to be interested in that doll, to care for it, bathe it, and so on. He did everything with the doll that I was doing with Petey.

"Chris was, still is, a very verbal child. He's always been very much center-stage. When Peter came, he really felt— well, I don't think he allowed himself to be displaced. And we were trying to protect him from being displaced, as well. Chris was so confident, we sensed he was going to hold his own pretty well.

"At that time we lived in a relatively isolated place. That was one of the reasons, I think, Chrissy was so eager for us to have a playmate for him. There were no other children around for him; in fact I had to 'import' children. But Peter came as something of a disappointment to Chris, because in spite of the fact that we kept saying we were going to bring home a *baby*, he expected his brother to be ready to play. I guess there was no way to prepare an eager three-year-old for the fact that this wasn't going to happen that way.

"Later there was a great deal of competition between the boys when Peter became mobile, when he was a person. Maybe he didn't know how to speak yet, but he certainly wanted his way and wanted to do the same things his big brother was doing. So he interfered with Chris a lot, went after his things, and disrupted what he was doing. They vied with each other for our attention, also vied over toys and belongings. And later, yes—the boys got into physical fights. I had a housekeeper at the time who sometimes made things better by making light of something, and sometimes made it worse. She always said she was just going to get boxing gloves and set them down and let them fight it out together. But we always had the rule, you know, 'I can't let you hurt this person.' You can have the rule, but that doesn't mean it's always going to work. So there was plenty of squabbling, and at times they'd get violent, or tried to get violent with each other.

"I can remember my mother visiting and saying, 'Well, you didn't see how it began.' And the truth is you don't see how a lot of things begin. So there are times when you simply have to go in and say, 'Look, this has to stop.' Sometimes you want to hear both sides of it, and sometimes what's going on is so unacceptable that the behavior simply has to be stopped. To protect everyone. . . .

"When Valerie, our third child, came along, Chris was seven and Peter was four. They've always had a different attitude with her—they're very protective toward her. For instance, one will correct the other for some kind of misbehavior with, 'Don't boss her around,' or 'What did you expect from her? She's little.' Probably because Valerie's the only girl, and the youngest, they have this special consideration. Even at four, I think Petey was old enough to realize that he was very big and powerful compared with his baby sister and that he had to be careful around her. And he still is. Maybe Valerie sees it differently—but I don't think so.

"Each of our kids is unique, but there are commonalities that they all share. Also, we try to do things separately with each of them when we can. We make time to go out with each one alone, as well as all together. In general, I think we're a family with deep commitments—and these seem to grow out of not just caring for each other, but fighting with each other and learning how to negotiate with each other, learning how to make up and also how to take the bumps that come along—how to take it all in stride. It's people learning how to live with other people. . . . That's the idea we'd like them to grow up with."

Ray C., father of Matthew, age six, and Ellie, age ten: "I can't remember how we told Ellie about the new baby—the exact words we used—except I do recall that we told her very early on. Some parents wait quite a while, until the mother really begins to show, but we felt it was important to tell Ellie, who was four, as soon as we knew ourselves. We figured she'd pick it up anyway from the other vibes around the house, from the conversation. And she did. So we told her early.

"I'm trying to picture it in my mind—I have a recollection that she was very excited at the news. She was doing a lot of doll-playing at the time, and that increased. She really loved taking care of her dolls. She also asked us some questions about babies, but not many.

"When Matthew was born—well, I can remember the actual night when Doris went into labor. We drove into the city to stay with some friends, and Doris's parents went up to stay with Ellie, who seemed pretty blasé at that time—didn't really have a sense of a big happening. But when we came home with Matthew, she was alternately excited, curious, and proud. I let her get on the phone to tell people. I'd dial, then I'd give her the phone, and she would tell everyone that she had a new baby brother.

"That was really exciting for her; she liked it because it gave her a way to participate in the event. But she clearly wasn't totally pleased about the arrival. She had many mixed feelings—like sometimes she wanted to do a swan dive right into the baby's bassinet! We found she'd become very active around the bassinet—acting up, making noise, trying to get our attention away from the baby. Of course she was showing some jealousy—we were prepared for it and we tried hard to give her extra attention, a lot of affection at that point. . . .

"Once we settled into a regular routine, Ellie calmed down. She didn't regress or get 'babyish,' but for a while she did act up whenever we fussed over Matthew. And later, when he started crawling around, she'd get impatient with him and march into her own room and slam the door very dramatically. I think it's tough on a first child—suddenly they have to come to terms with a whole new world. But she did come through it okay. She also sees now that she has a really big edge over Matt. She always will have, and he's reached the age where he looks up to her and admires her so much. She knows this and doesn't know it—I mean, she doesn't want to know it, somehow. Maybe she feels a sense of power, and that can be scary.

"They're ten and six now, and they compete a lot. They're always wrangling about what's 'fair'—whether Doris and I are being 'fair' or whether we're showing favoritism. We try hard to be evenhanded, to really be fair to both of them—though they don't always see it that way. . . .

"But they do surprise us sometimes. For instance, Ellie's an extremely capable reader, really loves it. Matt is getting there, but he's still a beginner. And there are times when he likes to be read to at night, and maybe we're too busy—so we ask Ellie if she'll read to him, and usually it's 'Oh, no! I haven't got time. No, I have homework!' or 'I can't be bothered!'—then there are other times when I'll walk into Matt's room, and they're both cuddled up on the bed and she's reading to him—and they've been that way for an hour! When Doris and I see that, well, it makes us feel good. It really does make up for a lot. . . ."

Laura T., mother of Allison, age seven, and Bruce, age twelve:
"Our family was in a peculiar situation because before Allison was born, I had been pregnant, and we'd had a baby, and that baby had died. So when I found out I was pregnant with Allison, it wasn't the first time that Brucie had been through a pregnancy, and a birth and a death—and that, I think, made a big difference in any negative feelings he might have had. He was old enough by then, he was over four, when I got pregnant again, and by then almost all the people he knew, all his friends, had brothers and sisters. He really thought that he was in some way unusual, being an only child, at that point. He really felt that way. I think also, having gone through the sad business with the other baby, about a year before—I think, because of that, having strong negative feelings would have been too fearful for him, although we've always been pretty open about any of our negative feelings. And compounded with all that was the fact

that we had just moved to a new house; we moved in the summer, in August, right before I got pregnant. So his whole life was in a bit of an uproar at that time. And he was more involved with the move than with my pregnancy—making new friends, getting established in the new neighborhood, and so on. . . .

"Alan and I told him right away, I think on the way back from the doctor's. I'm not very good at keeping secrets, so he would have guessed that something was going on—and been more curious about it anyway. So we told him right away; in fact, I had some trouble in the early days of the pregnancy and had to spend time in the hospital. So it was important for him to know, since he had been through a troublesome time before, and understood.

"I think I have a philosophy of life that is that we don't always pick the easiest things to do and we don't always know if they'll turn out right, but they're things we have to try. In any situation that Bruce faces, I've presented that kind of philosophy. And I presented my pregnancy that way. I said, 'Eventually I'm going to have a baby. And we don't know whether it's this time, or next time, or another time; but I'm going to keep trying until I have a baby. I'm going to stick with it.' I told him, 'It's like a family adventure. There'll be rough times, there'll be times when I don't feel well. We don't know what's going to happen. But you've got to try and work hard for the things you really want in life, and I really want another child.'

"We talked about the same thing in terms of his being fearful about learning to swim: 'You don't want to learn to swim, you're fearful about it; I'm a little fearful about going through another pregnancy. But you're going to end up wanting to learn to swim in your life, and I'm going to end up wanting another baby. And so we're both going to do this thing that's a little hard for us.'

"I feel that's really a good way to raise kids—to teach them to think about themselves and their own feelings, and also to get them to think about a parent's feelings. Not in the sense that you make them responsible for you, but so they know what's going on with their own mother and father. It helps us relate to one another—makes the relationship a two-way street.

"Bruce loved feeling the baby in my belly, listening to it. He even pretended he was talking to the baby; he'd make up little songs for it. When Allison was finally born, it wasn't traumatic for him or anything like that. I think we were all so happy that we actually had a baby, and a healthy one, that Brucie was genuinely very happy and excited. He didn't feel threatened, maybe because he knew lots of families in which there were two children, and he saw that those children got lots of love and attention, so I don't think that ever particularly worried him. Also, at his age, he'd moved out into the world and had a life of his own. He didn't feel like he needed his parents absolutely every minute. Obviously he didn't want to get cut out of the family in any way—who would, no matter what your age is?—but I don't think it ever occurred to him that having Allison meant he'd be ignored.

"I noticed, too, once a new child is born, parents look at the first child in a whole different way. The first child has been your baby right along—and suddenly that first child seems older. In the space of two days—before and after the birth—that little child will seem a lot bigger and stronger. Suddenly capable of hurting the younger child. I mean, parents have said to me that they see their older child as a 'menace'—suddenly capable of doing damage. And you can have very negative feelings toward this older child. So sibling rivalry, in a way, isn't all one-sided. It isn't just that the child might change—it's that the parents also might change in their perceptions of the first child. Parents do develop a very possessive feeling toward the new baby—they want to push everything away that comes between them. To me, this sets the stage for sibling rivalry as much as anything else. I think that's an important point.

"Another thing—I think kids have all sorts of expectations about the new baby, just as parents have expectations about what the family's supposed to be like when they have a second or a third child. You hear over and over that kids expect that baby to be a playmate or companion, and they're really angry that it isn't. So it might be a good idea to find out from the child what it is that they expect the baby to be like. Not to tell them, so much, as to just listen: 'When we have a baby, after the baby's born, what do you think you'll do with the baby? Have you thought about what the baby's going to look like?' If you can find out first what they expect, then you can help them to be more realistic. Take them to see other people with new babies; they'll see that babies are really tiny and wrinkled, and everybody's going to go around saying, 'The baby's so beautiful!' But the baby really isn't particularly beautiful to anyone else but the parents and relatives. Well, some babies are—but to a young child, a baby, a newborn baby, is not the baby in the magazine advertisements or on TV. So that's one small thing parents can do. Give them actual experiences being around new babies, also nursing mothers. It can help them to take a more realistic view, to cushion the shock a little, I think.

"Getting back to my own two—there wasn't much jealousy at first, but as Allison got older, things did change. I think it started when she became old enough to impinge on some of Bruce's privileges. Like, when she was old enough to sit up, I moved her into the front seat of the car, and Bruce into the backseat, because I needed a free hand while I was driving to give her a pacifier bottle, or to comfort her, or whatever. Bruce was pretty upset about being moved from the front to the backseat. That had always been his place, and he objected to that kind of change. I guess it seemed to him like a drop in his status. I don't know why things like that should bother kids—but they do.

"In general they get along pretty well these days. But they also compete with each other, and Bruce definitely doesn't like it when she seems to be encroaching on what *he* considers to be his special privileges. But because of their age difference, he has no trouble keeping ahead of her in most things. They squabble, yes—but as long as it's kept reasonable and there's no violence, that's okay. Alan and I try to be fair with both of them—but we can accept the battling. We battle too sometimes, right?''

CHAPTER
8

Love Is Not a Cookie Jar

Most of the time my three-year-old, Julie, plays quietly—
she's good as gold. But as soon as I start fussing over the
baby, feeding or cuddling him, Julie starts acting up and caus-
ing trouble. It's almost as if she can't bear my paying attention to the little one.

Siblings will compete with great zest in games and sports;
they will compete socially and creatively; and they will
squabble energetically over their belongings. But a more
subtle, more complex kind of competition is also going on:
competition for the love, attention, and approval of parents.
There is a deep need in children for this close involvement,
and those who can't get it through positive kinds of behavior
will often use negative means. We all know cases where kids
drain their parents of great amounts of concern and energy
simply by behaving badly enough. In short, kids will strive
one way or the other to gain parental attention.

This drive has its roots in a child's earliest instincts and
memories. A newborn baby is a helpless little creature, totally dependent on adults for every need. When mother and
father touch, hug, feed, change, talk to, or fuss over it, the
baby senses their complete focus of attention; at that point
the infant feels surrounded and protected by a coccoon of
loving care.

This feeling of exclusiveness—of being very special—is vital to a new baby, since it reinforces baby's sense of security and safety. But as the infant grows and siblings join the family constellation, the comfortable pattern changes: The older child begins to feel his or her specialness threatened by the newcomer.

SHARING THE PARENT

Sharing is a necessary part of everyday family life, and kids do learn, within limits, to share various belongings and activities. But one of the hardest lessons for a young sibling to learn is that parental care and love also have to be shared with sisters and brothers. Why do they resist? Why do siblings compete so doggedly for mother's or father's complete and exclusive attention? Psychologists, after years of study, have found a basic answer: To children, love is finite and limited. One authority likens the child's concept of love to a large pie. There are just so many slices to this pie, so if parents distribute the slices too freely, the pie will be gone.

Another image from a youngster's point of view is that of a cookie jar, and since a jar has limited capacity, its contents will eventually disappear. As sibling A sees it, every time Mommy or Daddy gives a cookie from the jar to sibling B, there will be one less cookie available for A. While this may seem oversimplified, it conveys the general thinking of many young children. As adults we can appreciate the uniqueness of parental love. We know that it is self-renewing and can never be "all used up." But this is a difficult concept for young children to grasp. Your role is to show each of your children that love isn't finite, that there's enough for all, that the "cookie supply" is indeed inexhaustible.

SIBLINGS AND SECURITY

We reassure our children most successfully by a sensitive combination of words and actions. Verbalizing problems with a child, drawing out his or her concerns, sharing our feelings, are vital parts of the process, but this has to be followed up by actions that are meaningful. It isn't enough to say to an older child, "We love the baby, but we love you, too, just as much," if the older sibling is then ignored, and parental time and attention are focused entirely on the new infant.

One mother was taken to task for devoting all of her concern and effort to a new baby and neglecting her four-year-old, Tommy. She shrugged off the criticism with, "Oh, Tommy knows I love him." But one is tempted to ask, "How does he know?" Kids are sensitive to parental behavior and quick to pick up and interpret subliminal messages. In this case—with mother's attention focused so obviously on the baby—Tommy may begin to feel that he no longer counts. Based on what he sees and senses, he may decide, rightly or not, that he's being shortchanged. To a four-year-old, hungry for his own share of attention, the message is that mother's love has been withdrawn and is now being invested elsewhere. The reaction is obvious: Tommy will become more and more disruptive and difficult in order to get attention, or he may withdraw into a shell of resentment.

Of course, a new baby or a sick child, for example, is entitled to extra care and concern—special needs certainly take precedence. But somehow a loving parent, no matter how busy, must find time for the needs of all the children in the family. In Tommy's case a special hug now and then, a little private conversation during breakfast or lunch, some minutes spent helping him with a new game or puzzle, can make all the difference. When father comes home from work, he might also give priority to a special visit with his son before getting involved with the baby. This becomes "Tommy's time," a little period set aside just for himself. This kind of attention—of consideration—tells the child that indeed he's valued and loved, along with the baby.

James L., a young businessman and father of two small children, deals with this very consciously:

> Every day, when I come home from work, I kiss Ellen hello, look in on Sue, our new baby (she's five months), then Timmy and I sit down for our "special time" together. He's three and a half, still a little uncertain about the baby. Has kind of mixed feelings. So Timmy and I have our own half hour or so. We sit in the den together, and he climbs up in my lap, or sometimes just sits next to me, and we have a good man-to-man visit. I hear all about his day, what he did, who he saw, where he went. Sometimes we look at a book together. Then we both go in and visit Sue for a few minutes, until it's time to get ready for dinner. Timmy really looks forward to these little private sessions—and you know, so do I.

Actually the tug-of-war for parental time isn't very severe with a new baby in the house. Babies are passive, and do sleep a lot, which allows parents to devote themselves more freely to the others. But when baby becomes a toddler, the problems can intensify. Active toddlers are like sponges that sop up every moment of a harassed parent's time. So it's more important than ever for parents to be aware of the needs, and rights, of the older siblings for a fair share of their attention.

This is a tall order, but far from impossible. One mother with a two-and-a-half-year-old toddler, Jane, and a six-year-old daughter, Nina, found a simple but workable solution. She encouraged Nina to help her with various cooking projects. At those times when the toddler was napping or playing quietly (at least for the moment), Mother and Nina would spend time together in the kitchen baking bread, making desserts, and so on. This gave Nina a rich sense of being helpful and of participating in an interesting project with a parent. She also felt proud of herself, since she was doing something "grown up," far beyond the limited capacities of her baby sister.

THE SICK CHILD

When one of your children gets sick, a shift in priorities is required. Sick children are of course entitled to a great deal of extra time and attention, and their siblings have to be understanding of the problem and the reasons for Mother's or Father's preoccupations.

Illness in the family is in fact a learning experience for all the kids. And it can be a reassuring one: A young child who sees parents caring for a sick brother or sister, or one who perhaps has had an accident, learns about parental resources and responsibility. It comforts the well child to realize that he or she, too, in the event of illness, will be properly and lovingly cared for.

If a child is bedridden for any length of time, chances are he or she will receive books, toys, and games from sympathetic friends and relatives. It's a good idea to keep your other siblings' needs in mind. It will make them feel less neglected if now and then they also receive a new book or a small toy. Siblings can also be helpful in tending the bedridden one, carrying lunch trays, keeping the patient company, and so on. Where it's feasible, all members of the family can participate in the ministering process. Nothing pleases a youngster more than to have a parent say, "Daddy and I really appreciate the way you're cooperating now that Billy's sick. You've been a real help."

QUALITY VERSUS QUANTITY

If love isn't a cookie jar, it isn't a time clock either. Sharing and apportioning affection among your children isn't a question of following a rigid time plan. In other words, you don't have to think, "I've given fourteen minutes of attention to one, now I must give fourteen minutes of attention to the other."

We know from our own experience as adults that real love can't be measured by the ticking of a clock. Nor do our children expect this kind of parental behavior. With siblings, although time does play a part, it is the quality of parental attention that matters most. Child psychologist Haim Ginott writes, "Children do not yearn for equal shares of love: they need to be loved uniquely, not uniformly. The emphasis is on quality, not quantity."

A parent who leans over backward to be superfair in dealing with each child may wind up resenting all of them. No parent can give every child the exact same number of hugs and kisses or precisely the same words of affection at all times. That kind of rigidity misses the point. Affection can't be forced, and love can't be ladled out like a commodity. The parent who tries to keep a scorecard will wind up in a trap, because being "absolutely fair" isn't the same thing as being "absolutely loving." What kids do need and want to know is that their parents care about them. They also need to feel that this concern will not be diminished by the arrival of a new sibling.

What most children worry over intuitively is the loss of love *plus* the loss of access to their parent's concern. So, for their own security and peace of mind, kids have to sense deeply that mother and/or father will always be there when needed. But remember that youngsters have to be shown, not just told. What counts here aren't words so much as actions—the tangible quality of the attention you bring personally to each of your siblings.

When Harry K. takes his little girl, Jill, for an outing in the park or to the movies, he is with her fully. For that period, Jill feels that she's her father's only daughter. When Linda M. takes her son, Peter, shopping with her or to a museum, Peter feels that he's his mother's only son. These parents know how to focus completely on the child they are with. As Dr. Ginott puts it, "For the moment to be memorable, our attention must be undivided."

Of course, there are no perfect solutions; even in the best and most caring of families, competition for parental love will go on and on. Some children will always need more overt attention than others. And differences in temperament and personality will also play a part in how our kids respond to affection. Similarly, we can't love each of our children in exactly the same manner, since each is uniquely human in his or her own way.

The sibling power struggle is a natural one—part of a child's need to learn, test, and grow. The parent's loving response must also be natural. By showing our special concern for each youngster, by enriching our moments with every child as a unique individual, we can convey the all-important message that indeed each sibling truly matters.

A FEW SUGGESTIONS

To help in dealing with sibling competition, here are a few hints and guidelines, based on the findings of authorities and the material in the preceding chapters.

- Don't be upset or feel you and your spouse are doing a poor job because your siblings squabble. It's a natural part of life and growth for them to fight, make up—and start fighting again.
- Don't interfere in sibling arguments. Try to stay out unless the squabbling becomes violent. Kids develop confidence and self-reliance when they learn to settle their quarrels by themselves.
- Don't allow your siblings to draw you into their endless wrangles or to play one parent against the other. Kids will try to manipulate parents if they can, which sets up harmful and negative patterns.
- Don't try to be a referee or a judge. Taking sides is a no-win situation that only feeds the competition and leaves you open to charges of favoritism. When a decision does have to be made, keep it short and to the point.
- Don't tolerate any violence in your family, either physical or verbal. No matter how much your siblings may squabble, "no violence" should be a hard-and-fast rule.
- Don't hang labels on your kids such as "sloppy" or

"lazy" or "brainy." It doesn't matter if these labels are favorable or unfavorable—they act as uncalled-for judgments and can put unfair pressure on your youngsters.

· Don't judge your children's behavior according to the perceptions and memories you have of your own childhood. Your kids aren't you, nor is their world a carbon copy of the world in which you yourself grew up.

· Don't make comparisons between siblings or plague them with remarks such as, "Why can't you stay neat like your little sister?" or "Why aren't you as polite as your big brother?" Such questions rarely generate results—only resentments.

· Don't put heavy pressure on your kids to measure up to your expectations or set unrealistic competitive goals for them, physical or mental. Remember to think of their ego needs, not your own.

· Don't shortchange one sibling because of the heavy demands made by another. Whatever the demands on your time, remember that each of your children needs a healthy share of concern, love, and attention.

And now for the positive—

· Do keep out of your siblings' wrangles whenever possible. When intervention is necessary, get to the bottom of the problem without endless soul-searching about pleasing everyone or trying to be always "100 percent fair." When intervening, keep the needs of the children uppermost.

· Do separate your siblings whenever violence breaks out, and keep them firmly apart until they quiet down. You can threaten punishment, too—but if you follow through on this, be sure not to contradict yourself by resorting to violence or verbal abuse on your wrongdoers!

· Do make firm, clear rules for your family's behavior, but after these are established, avoid moralizing about them. Moralizing only stirs up unnecessary feelings of guilt.

· Do try to anticipate the trouble spots. Try to pick up on

"danger signals" and break up any bad combinations of kids ahead of time, if and when you can.

· Do protect your siblings against each other when it's necessary. At times the littler ones may need protection against the bigger ones—and the reverse also holds true!

· Do try a little behavior modification, rewarding and encouraging good behavior and attitudes. Instead of simply ruling out bad behavior, try to couple this with positive suggestions and helpful alternatives.

· Do encourage your kids in areas where they show special physical and creative abilities—as long as these interests aren't pursued to the exclusion of everything else.

· Do encourage each of your siblings to make use of talents and skills in his or her own way, without being compared favorably or unfavorably with the other siblings in the family.

· Do reassure your younger children that someday they, too, will be big enough to have all the privileges and prerogatives enjoyed by the older ones. Meanwhile, point out the advantages they enjoy now.

· Do make certain that each of your siblings has his or her own private place for keeping personal toys, books, clothes, and other belongings. And do convey at the same time that you and the family respect their rights to these possessions.

· Do show your feelings with actions, not only words. Spend enough personal time with each of your siblings— alone with each when possible. At these times, try to be with each child fully and honestly, treating him or her as unique, special, and loved.

A Father's Diary: Or, How I Grew Closer to My Daughter When My Son Was Born by James A. Levine

October 31
9:30 P.M.

Joshua was born yesterday—12:37 A.M. to be exact.

I'm bleary from the lack of sleep, the crush of phone calls from well-wishers, and the needs of four-year-old Jessica for some special attention of her own. I'm much less anxious, though, this second time around. Because I know what it's like to be a father, I'm not so preoccupied with myself. I'm able now to attend to the reactions of others—relatives, neighbors, Joan, and especially Jessica.

Last time, of course, there was no Jessica. Now, more than ever, I find it fascinating to watch the world through her eyes. I don't really know Joshua yet, but in a sense I've been developing my intimacy with him for the last nine months, through Jessica.

Reprinted by permission of James A. Levine. Mr. Levine, of the Bank Street College of Education in New York City, is the author of *Who Will Raise the Children? New Options for Fathers (and Mothers)* [Lippincott, 1976], which won the Family Life Book Award of the Child Study Association of America.

Jessica knew about "the baby" almost as soon as we did. We had read her all the appropriate "where babies come from" books, explaining in simple but accurate terms how she had come to life. But something must have gotten lost in the translation: One day Jessica proclaimed with assurance that, when Joan and I went to the hospital, the sperm would meet the egg; then, after a few days, we'd all go to pick the baby up.

During Joan's second trimester, Jessica embarked on three months of fantasy play about babies. Everything in the house was a baby: Not only her twenty-three assorted stuffed animals and dolls, but the spoons (they were babies compared with the forks), the juice glasses (they were babies compared with the milk glasses), and especially Joan and me. Jessica was constatnly taking care of us, ministering in baby talk to our needs: "Don't worry, baby, Mommy will take care of you," or "It's all right, baby, Daddy's here."

She was always mommy or daddy—or baby. When she wasn't taking care of us, she made it clear that *she* wanted to be taken care of. Three and a half years old, she would crawl on the floor and ask if she could have a pacifier, eat with a baby spoon, and would want Joan to nurse her.

A director in charge of a very important script, she'd walk around the house issuing assignments: "Dad, you're the mom; Mom, you're the big sister; I'm the dad." Convinced of the realism of her own casting, she would often assign me a part ("Dad, you're the baby") and then break her dramatic spell in order to ask me a question—"Dad, you're the dad again for a minute; can I have a glass of milk?"

By the seventh month of Joan's pregnancy, Jessica was back to playing big sister and issuing different types of edicts. She was more comfortable with the prospect of the new arrival and really wanted in on it: "Dad, I want a baby brother; we're going to name him Billy." Two days later, "Dad, I decided his name is Max." For a while, she had a strong sense of symmetry: "Two boys and two girls, that will be nice."

But as the due date approached—and as we prepared her

for the lack of control we or she had over the newborn's sex, assuring her that we would love whatever we got, just as we loved and would always love her—she decided she definitely wanted a girl: "Three girls and one boy in the family. That would be good. We'll name her Peter."

Well, "Peter" wasn't a girl and he wasn't a Peter. When I told Jessica about Joshua, some seven and a half hours after his birth, she seemed disappointed: "I thought we were going to have a girl." Of course, she might well have been disappointed at whatever we had. When friends brought over a bassinet on the day when Joan began very mild labor, Jessica wasn't terribly interested. This four-year-old, who all her life was attracted with something like a magnetic force to babies, bassinets, cribs, and carriages, couldn't have been less concerned! It was straight out of the textbooks.

The trick, I knew, was not only to respect her feelings but to try to include her in some of the excitement that she couldn't help but feel emanating from me. I explained that I was going to call some friends and relatives and invited her to dial all the phone numbers; if she wanted to, she could announce the news. The feeling of power a four-year-old gets from using the telephone helped her feel secure enough to start sharing: "Hello, is John or Kitty there? . . . Kitty, *I* have a baby brother . . . Joshua Lawrence!"

For Jessica, Joshua's birthday was a day of confrontation with a new meaning of big and little—Jessica and Joshua. There were ups and downs—pride on the telephone and at school, but also a mysterious earache and a dinnertime temper tantrum. After dinner, she went to the baby's chest of drawers and pulled out a receiving blanket to cover herself with while we read a book. From a living-room table cluttered with books she picked out three for us to read together, all appropriate for helping her cope with Joshua's homecoming: *Grownups Cry Too, Joshua's Day,* and *Tell Me a Mitzi,* one of our family favorites, a warm and humorous book about Mitzi and her baby brother, a book in which one thing is for sure—he's the baby and *she's* in charge!

Jessica's expectation of a relationship with another member of the family has added another dimension to her life, and to my relationship with her. She has revealed, and I have attempted to know more intimately, not only her anxieties and insecurities but, above all, her incredibly able and clever ways of coming to terms with the unknown, of establishing her own personhood.

The only sad part of Joshua's arrival has been the almost universal glee of others that we had a boy. The comments have been endless: "Oh, you're so lucky it's a boy; now you won't have to have another one" (we weren't planning to); "I bet that's just what you *really* wanted: (no, much to everybody's disbelief, what we *really* hoped for was a healthy baby); "Now you'll have a child for yourself" (as if somehow Jessica was not fully mine? Visions of Josh and me going hunting in the wilds or off to wrestling matches at Madison Square Garden?).

I am delighted that Joshua is here, though not for any of the reasons attributed to me by others. I delight in trying to see the world through Jessica's eyes and in trying to let her see it through mine. I am delighted at the prospect of doing the same with Joshua. But I'm sad, and a little bit hurt, by the automatic celebration of his sex, as if it gives him something that Jessica doesn't have, or me something that I don't already have with her. Jessica is perhaps too young to be hurt by the subtle and unintentional way in which the world's greeting of her brother reflects its assessment of her own sex. Most of the well-wishers do mean well; they are unaware, I suppose, of what they imply. After all, how could they know—as I do—who Jessica is and what she means to me?

10

Special Occasions, Special People

Our three kids have their share of fights, which is okay, reasonable; Ted and I can live with that. But when it gets rough is when something special comes up—you know, a birthday, a sleep-away visit, so on. Then the jealousy *really* starts!

In most families, special events and occasions are times when sibling rivalry seems emphasized, especially the more negative aspects. But a little foresight and planning can help to ease difficulties and strengthen some of the positives.

BIRTHDAYS

A birthday is certainly cause for celebration, especially for your birthday child. But what about his or her siblings? Let's listen to a few of their complaints:

Josh B., age six:

My older brother, Pete, has fun birthdays. He chooses neat things to do—takes friends bowling or to the movies, has them for sleepover, goes to the amusement part. And I can't go with them. He says I'm too young. I'd be a pest. He says older kids don't want little kids hanging around. He says it's *his* birthday; for once he doesn't have to have me along.

Gail T., age ten:

> When I had my last birthday, my three-year-old kid sister, Pesty Paula, butted in. She was supposed to stay with the baby-sitter, but she kept getting away. We'd be in the middle of a game, and in she'd come. "I wanna play too!" she'd yell. Then the baby-sitter would come and take her away, kicking and screaming. When we were having cake and ice cream, in she'd come again, grabbing food, making a racket. Some of my friends laughed, but I was very embarrassed.

Josh B.'s parents always tried to treat each of their sons fairly. Josh, too, was allowed to choose "fun things" for *his* birthday celebration. But what they forgot to do was to provide some satisfactory activity or outlet for the noncelebrant. Josh, for instance, might have gone to a movie or other entertainment with an older relative or friend. Pete, in his turn, should have similar arrangements made for him. Another alternative for the older sib can be to have him help out at the younger one's party.

In Gail's case, the family did make an attempt to ensure "Pesty Paula's" absence. Unfortunately the baby-sitter wasn't able or interested enough to keep Paula occupied. Next time, more careful plans could be made to keep the little one out of the way.

What about those lucky siblings for whom brother's or sister's birthdays are pleasurable times?

Tyrone D., age 10:

> I had fun at Sean's sixth birthday party. He and I worked on it the day before. I hung streamers and blew up balloons. Sean decorated paper napkins and wrote kids' names on the candy cups. I helped him with the spelling. At the party, I was in charge of games like Pin the Tail on the Donkey. All the little kids wanted me to spin them around. I thought up forfeits, too. And ate the most ice cream.

Maria V., age five:

> I love when Marc and Sonia [her older siblings] have a birth-
> day, because I get to go to Grandpa and Aunt Lillian's house.
> We make cookies, or I help Grandpa make a birdhouse. Or
> plant in my very own garden. I took Fuzzy for a walk all by
> myself. And once we all went for a ride on the lake!

Tyrone's parents encouraged their older sib not only to help
in the preparations for the younger one's party, but to join in
the party itself. In Maria's case, they made sure that she, too,
would have an enjoyable day, visiting favorite relatives.

Both these families obviously managed to strengthen their
siblings' relationships positively, before any birthday problems surfaced. So neither Tyrone nor Maria showed evidence
of jealousy or of feeling left out. Parents with this kind of
positive, commonsense approach to sibling rivalry can usually weather birthday "crises" and the upsets associated with
other similar special occasions. All it takes is a little thought
and planning.

TRIPS AND VACATIONS

FATHER: How about Lake Sagamore for our next
vacation? Great fishing, and there's a beach
for the kids.

DAVID, AGE 10: There's nothing to do there. Only fish all
day. And the water's too shallow. It's for
babies!

SARA, AGE 6: It is not! It's just right.

MOTHER: What about Mount Shiloh?

DAVID: Hey, that's a neat place! They've got video
games and a bike track.

SARA: But they don't have a beach, only a pool.
And it's too deep for me.

Sara and David's parents faced a typical problem, that of families
trying to plan a holiday trip and attempting to satisfy everybody.

Aware of the opposing needs of their siblings, they came up with a compromise. Another spot on the lake was chosen that had both a beach and a deep-water raft and also offered a nearby amusement park. Both children were satisfied. In sum, to minimize rivalry and discontent, parents do have to weigh the needs of all the kids involved. Naturally *you* make the final vacation decision, but a bit of forethought and fair planning can alleviate rivalries that might otherwise crop up.

The process of getting to your vacation spot has its own minor pitfalls. Whether by car, bus, or plane, arguments often arise as to who will have the "best" seat. Squabbling about having the front or middle seat in a car is a well-known hassle in many families.

Fred N., a Dallas father of three, recalls one recent outing:

> The kids, Timmy, Suzanne, and Patty, our youngest, had to share the backseat. Luckily they couldn't argue about sitting in front, because Mom was immoveably there. So first Timmy and Suzanne grabbed the window places, leaving the baby in the middle. Before we'd gone two miles, she was carrying on because she couldn't see out. So we made Suzanne take Patty's place, with the agreement that Timmy would change with her soon. This brought a lull, but it didn't last. The wrangling started up again—whoever was in the middle felt deprived. Finally I had to threaten to turn around and go home again if they didn't behave. And that worked.

This particular family could have had an easier trip if Mom and Dad had made a few simple plans ahead of time. Some suggestions:

- Agree beforehand on *who* will sit *where,* and for how long.
- Agree on games that everyone can play.
- If the youngest falls asleep, decide what the older sibs can play quietly.
- Announce what places will be rest stops.
- Announce that there will be periods of solitary and *silent* play.

- Ask (and help) each child to pack his or her own tote bag, filled with favorite toys, games, and books.
- Be sure any necessary travel companions (stuffed toy, security blanket, and so on) are included.
- Pack a "survival bag" with items such as tissues, wet-wipes, Band-Aids, safety pins, Thermos of juice, and snacks.

That kind of preparation can defuse the more violent explosions of rivalry and help make your trip enjoyable.

GET-TOGETHERS/VISITING RELATIONS

A family get-together may involve visiting relatives, outside your own home. Getting there may necessitate using some of the preceding tips; but staying there may need other kinds of preparation to foresee and forestall in-family squabbling.

First, talk to your hosts ahead of time in order to

- Find out what other children will be present, and their ages.
- Find out what the hosts want the kids to do, where they want them to play, to eat, and so on.
- Offer to bring games, toys, or other contributions to your kids' enjoyment.
- Offer any necessary information about your children, such as Penny's need to nap, Henry's shyness with strangers, Philip's food allergies, and so on.
- If necessary, bring along any special food that may be needed.

Now talk to your own kids about their "visiting behavior." Help them to accept the dictum, "When in Rome, do as the Romans do."

- Assure shy Henry you'll be close by.
- Discuss what Grandma (aunt, uncle, cousin) will expect of them. Polite hellos? No roughhousing indoors? No fighting among themselves? Being friendly to other kids?
- Clue them in to the various people they'll meet. Try to say positive things about Aunt Virginia, Cousin Joe, Un-

cle Russell. Reassure them that they won't have to spend *all* their time with the grown-ups.

· If your children are old enough, they might also get a kick out of sketching a family tree.

If the occasion means that family members are coming to *your* house, use the same tips in planning with the children how to act as hosts. Your youngsters will be more comfortable if the party is at home. They may also be uninhibited, more apt to show off or get wild. So they should know that poor behavior will lead to punishment—banishment to their rooms, an end to the games, separation from their siblings, and so on. But if fair rules are set beforehand, chances are that special-occasion manners will save the day.

Grandparents and Grandchildren

Many families are lucky in having one or two favorite relations—cousins, aunts, uncles, even that special person who becomes an aunt or uncle by "adoption" because of their loving relationships with your children.

These favorite people take the role of surrogate parents at times and can often quell sibling outbursts more efficiently than anyone else. Why? Perhaps because the children don't want to lose the respect of this special adult. Maybe the children don't feel the usual pressures of day-to-day living with them. Or perhaps it's because aunt, uncle, or cousin simply have stronger rules against squabbling.

Children do feel able to develop relationships with beloved family members such as Aunt Mary or Cousin Tom—relationships that differ from those they have with their own parents. Aunt Mary just seems to have more time to listen, to sympathize, to comfort. Cousin Tom always takes them on fascinating hikes or helps them to build airplane models and dollhouses.

But the most important family members, next to their own parents, are usually the siblings' grandparents. These are the direct progenitors of the family, also the bulwark for their immediate descendants. And grandparents often play a major role in dealing with matters of sibling rivalry. This is what two different grandchildren say:

Jamie, age eight, the middle of three siblings:

> I love to visit Grandma and Grandpa. He always says, "Jamie, you really are Somebody!" He lets me help him in his workshop, he doesn't fuss when I break a piece of wood. And he's not always telling me how messy I am. Grandpa listens when I talk to him—really listens, I mean. Grandma fusses over me. She stops to give me a hug when she's rushing around, asks me what dessert I want, and is always ready to play games—not baseball, I mean, board games like checkers or even Monopoly.

Sonia, the older of two children, says,

> I don't like to visit my grandparents, so I'm glad we don't go very often. They're so strict. Grandpa says we make too much noise. Grandma is always comparing me with my mother when she was my age. "Your mother didn't fuss about food the way you do, Sonia. She always ate everything I gave her." (Mother says that's not so!) And Grandma isn't fair—she lets my little sister, Lara, get away with murder. If I did what Lara does in Grandma's house, I'd be in big trouble!

Two families, two kinds of grandparents, and both have a lasting effect on their grandchildren. A third group of grandparents may have little or no effect on grandchildren at all. These may have more or less abdicated their roles by moving to a distant retirement community or by adopting the philosophy, "I've raised my kids; now let them raise theirs." By thus cutting basic age-old family connections, they may shortchange themselves and their grandchildren, to the detriment of both.

"Great-Parenting"

Jamie's grandparents have opted to keep the close connection that their role has always meant and thus play a vital part in the lives of their grandchildren. One step removed from daily parental concerns of providing for the needs of the children—with all the problems of supporting and raising a family—grandparents have the chance to see each child as an individual with his or her own needs, anxieties, and abilities. Jamie's grandfather, sensing Jamie's feelings of inferiority as a "middle child" in the family structure, gives him a feeling of self-worth by admiring him, sharing with him, having time to "really listen." Grandmother, too, by physically expressing her delight in his presence and her willingness to enter Jamie's activities, reassures the boy of her deep love.

Erik Erikson, the noted psychologist, says that to achieve true maturity is to have concern for establishing and guiding the young, which he calls "generativity." He also points out that many fail to achieve this by entering a period of stagnation rather than achieving growth. Stagnation, he claims, arises from excessive concentration on self.

Grandparents will have a strong influence on easing sibling rivalry if they are like Jamie's grandparents. Dr. Arthur Kornholder calls this effective role "great-parenting," which especially nurtures grandchildren. In fact, grandchildren often get along with such relatives *better* than they do with their own parents, and vice versa. There are logical reasons for this:

- There's a calming distance between grandparent and child, removed from the day-to-day problems of growing up in a shared home.
- Grandparents, relieved of the immediate necessities, can concentrate on the child's strengths and problems.
- Grandparents can take a long-range view of the child's growth problems.
- Caring grandparents can help ease the strife that arises from sibling pressures.

Jennifer K. talks about her grandparents:

I really like to go to see Gram and Pops (that's what I call my grandparents). They live about ten blocks away from us, and

I usually visit them a couple of times a week. They always seem to want me and don't bug me. At home, my kid sisters are always hanging around me—at times I think I hate them! They get into my things and pester me for attention. Mom and Dad both work, and old Mrs. R—— lets the kids get their own way. When I yell at them, my parents say that because I'm the oldest, I should know better. But Gram and Pops understand. They don't scold me. Actually, when I go home from their house, I'm nicer to my little sisters—they aren't really so bad. And Gram and Pops say they'll grow up after a while.

Most grandparents who exemplify this positive kind of "great-parenting" have done several things:

- They have an ongoing commitment to family. They remember birthdays, special occasions, keep lines of communication open by letter or in person. They are available in times of need and illness, birth and death. They are the strong "bottom line" in the family structure.
- They maintain a time and place for family as a whole, as well as for individual members. They don't denigrate one member to others in the family. They are truly concerned and interested in their grandchildren; and never betray personal confidences.
- Their outlook and actions are altruistic. Rather than feeling deprived and lonely because of advancing age or infirmity, they look outward to the needs of the family and do try to help *when asked to.*

Grandparents can not only be supportive of siblings but can offer them a perspective different from that of their parents. One young grandson, Toby, says,

At home, my big brother, Greg, and I fight a lot. He teases me, makes fun of my friends and what I do. That gets me mad, and I sock him. Then my parents butt in and yell at both of us. They tell Greg he's old enough to know better, that he should be an example to me. So that makes *him* mad, and he gets even with me later. But we're different at my grand-parents' house. They just say, *"No* fighting here." And they mean it. Grandmom and Grandpop don't excuse us or blame us or play favorites. They expect us to behave. I have to say it's nice, 'cause Greg and I get along there. Somehow he doesn't tease me, and I don't feel like always fighting him. Going to our grandparents' is like a vacation.

Visiting grandparents is taking one small step outside the nuclear family unit—a step into a wider world. So here rivalrous siblings have an opportunity perhaps to act in a way more suitable to society-at-large.

This, finally, may be the most important ingredient in grandparenting: to pass on an integrated caring sense of fam-ily structure in a society that truly needs it.

11

Matched Sets

Linda and I were identical twins, so we were always made to feel unique and special. Which had its good and its bad sides. People were constantly treating us as a pair of dolls, never as individuals. And when it came to getting attention—well, I think our younger brother, Peter, was really shortchanged!

The novelist John Barth is half of a set of opposite-sex twins. At the time he and his sister were born, their brother was three years old. When told that Mommy had just given birth to twins, the little boy nodded thoughtfully and announced, Now we have a Jack and a Jill." Barth wrote later, "We were a Jack and Jill indeed, between whom everything went without saying." This close bonding, which included their own private language, went on until the Barth twins reached their teens and were placed in different high school curricula, at which point they began to develop in different directions.

Of all sib relationships, none is quite so novel and unique as that of twin children. They are a combination that is completely different from any other two siblings.

IDENTICAL AND FRATERNAL TWINS

Before looking at these specific qualities and differences, let's note some definitions:

Identical twins are the result of a single egg that divided upon being fertilized. Identical twins, coming from the same genetic source, are always of the same sex. The scientific name for this is *monozygotic*.

Fraternal twins are the result of two separate eggs that are fertilized simultaneously and that then develop together in the womb. Fraternal twins may be of the same or opposite sexes. The scientific term for this is *dizygotic*.

It is with identical twins that we find the closest similarities, both physical and temperamental. They tend to look alike, sound alike, and to develop in similar ways. Identical twins have the same blood types, same facial features, same general coloring of eyes and hair, even the same kind of fingerprints. These are the youngsters of whom we often hear people say, "You can't tell them apart." Fraternal twins, on the other hand, usually have definite physical differences. They may be of the same sex or of opposite sex, but in either case these two can be told apart fairly easily. Like all kids, fraternal twins will probably grow up with different personalities, skills, interests, likes, and dislikes.

As with birth order in families, being part of a set of twins has certain advantages and certain drawbacks.

Advantages
Whether identical or fraternal, twins have a built-in, ready-made companion—another person whose life experience is shared right from the womb itself. Twins generally like and accept each other, and (particularly in the early years) have a relationship with less friction and squabbling than do non-twin siblings. If there are other kids in the family, either younger or older, twins are usually less involved with them and content to be with each other. In their world, "two's company" is an adage with real meaning.

Terry and Conrad B., parents of identical twin boys, had this to say:

Right from the start, Alan and Mark got on well, with a

minimum of friction. They weren't only close in age, they were the exact *same* age—yet it didn't seem to bother them. Oh, they scrapped a little, but never very badly or for very long. In a few minutes it was all over. When the baby, Molly, came along, they were four and a half. They liked her but never got very involved with her doings. She didn't pose any sibling threat because, I guess, they thought of themselves as a team. Growing up, they rarely had trouble with other kids; for them it was always two to one!

Anyone who's ever seen adults oohing and aahing over a pair of charming look-alikes in a stroller can readily spot another advantage: Twins enjoy a special status, both in the family and outside it. According to statistics, the chance of a twin birth is roughly one in ninety, so these children aren't commonplace. Identical twins, small mirror images of each other, appealing and lovable, are bound to arouse interest and attention. One half of a "matched set" said recently. "When we were kids, our mother always dressed us identically. Everyone always made a big fuss over us—parents, grandparents, other relatives, even teachers. Being the center of attention made us feel pretty important. And the interesting thing about all this attention is that we didn't have to do anything to earn it."

As we've seen, all kids want to feel unique; all kids are hungry for parental love and approval. With twins, under normal family circumstances, this usually happens automatically. There is a kind of prestige involved in twinship. As a result, whatever the stresses and strains of later years, twins often begin life with a psychological head start—a feeling of being truly special.

Twins also have the experience of consistent sharing. Whereas single children in the birth order have to learn to share with their siblings, this comes naturally to twins. From the moment of birth they will share parents and parental security. Later, as they grow, they will share the problems of childhood and can face the outside world as a team. This intimate relationship, plus the uniqueness of their status, gives twins an added level of strength. But it isn't an unmixed blessing. Being in a close sibling twosome does have its drawbacks as well.

Disadvantages
Twins are almost always being compared with each other, not only at home, but in school, at camp, and on the playground—even on the street, where total strangers will happily join in!

However well-meaning and enthusiastic it may be, this constant comparison—measuring one twin against the other—is a form of judgment and can heighten feelings of jealousy and competition. This is especially true of fraternal twins, where there are likely to be greater variations in size, strength, and mental ability between the children. Comparison is a burden that most twins learn to live with, but it can at times be subtly harmful to the young child's developing self-confidence.

Years ago parents tended to treat twins as cute playthings. There was great emphasis on dressing twins alike, treating them alike, and encouraging them to do everything in exactly the same way. Twins, particularly identical ones, were each treated as merely half of a single unit, which could and did lead to identity confusion. Today's parents, more sensitive and knowledgeable, usually try to downplay the "oneness" of twins and to encourage each to develop as a normal, distinct individual. In this way the bonding—which will always remain crucial and important—can be tempered and balanced.

Because twins are constantly together and follow their natural urge to share most growing experiences, they often develop great dependency on each other and may feel insecure when separated. In some cases, young twins will cry and express deep anxiety when apart, even for a short while. Although these are extreme examples, they point up pitfalls. Mutual dependency, especially among identical or fraternal twins of the same sex, can be carried to a point where, later in life, they may have difficulty in marrying or in choosing independent careers. In these cases, twins simply don't wish to face life without each other. Closely bonded pairs sometimes marry other twins and often choose similar jobs or professions—at which, incidentally, they may enjoy great success. Ann Landers and her twin sister, Abigail Van Buren (known as "Dear Abby") are good examples. Though working independently of each other, both women have won equal success as family-advice columnists.

Where the dependency is extreme, however, twins may checkmate each other, leaning together, avoiding challenges, shunning the outside world. But those are the exceptions. Generally, twins can and do grow up normally and function very well both as children and as adults.

TWINS AND SIBLING RIVALRY

Young twin children are like kids everywhere. They have the same need for parental affection, self-esteem, a sense of achievement—also the same stirrings of jealousy and rivalry.

Jud and Robby M. are identical twins, so alike that at first even their parents had a hard time telling them apart. When they were babies and toddlers, their mother dressed them alike; later there were variations—each boy had his own favorite coat, sweater, and so on, and they were encouraged to select different colors. But even when given options, they generally chose similar clothes and enjoyed the same books, toys, TV programs, and outdoor activities.

The boys, slight of stature, good-looking, somewhat quiet-mannered, got on well together. There was some fighting and squabbling, but there were no explosions or violent outbursts. Their differences, like their temperaments, were muted. Later in life they made an effort to change their mirror-image appearance. Jud now has a beard. Robby combs his hair in a different style. And each has his own style of dressing. Characteristically, the two young men went into the same profession—filmmaking—and each is having success. Although they work for different companies and are geographically far apart, each one is making almost the same identical progress up the professional ladder!

"We're still close," says Robby, "and I guess we always will be. We talk to each other on the phone a lot, compare notes, exchange news about the industry. It's funny—we've always been rivals, but we've also been supportive of each other. I guess you could say we're 'support rivals.' That's what we are—competitors who give each other a lot of backup."

The concept of "support rivals" symbolizes the sibling relationship between most identical twins. While they still have all the natural competitive drives, their inherent close-ness and twin-sufficiency gives this rivalry a unique under-pinning of mutual, wholehearted support.

Another personality factor plays its part here. Studies show that among identical twins, one will often assume a dominant role, whereas the other remains the passive part-ner. Sally T. says of herself and her twin sister, "Nancy was always the aggressor. She took the lead and made the deci-sions—what games we'd play, what friends we'd have, and so on. I usually went along, whatever it was. But I don't recall ever feeling any resentment, because we always wanted the same things *anyway*. Now that we're adults, it's not so apparent, but I think I still lean on her advice more than she does on mine." The active-passive relationship is prevalent in many identical-twin relationships, creating a kind of mutual compatibility that is comfortable for both youngsters.

This is not generally the case for fraternal twins. Here, while pair-bonding is important, each child has distinctive qualities that aren't necessarily matched by the other. Frater-nal twins usually do not look alike, nor do they think or act alike. Rivalry between fraternal twins—especially opposite-sex pairs—is much like rivalry between any two children in the family. There are the usual battles over toys, clothes, cookies, who gets to pick the TV show, and so forth. Be-cause they are twins, they may be expected to share many toys and possessions; but a constant need to share everything can cause anger and intensify the rivalry. So it's important, where possible, to see that each twin has his or her own separate playthings in addition to those that are used jointly.

Between twins, there is another significant variation on the typical themes of sibling rivalry. Since there's no age difference, and the twins will share experiences more or less jointly, there's no envy based on the privileges that accompany childhood age spans. With fraternal twins, both are old enough at the same time to ride a bike, to start nursery school, to stay up later at night, and so on. This has a natural leavening influence and tends to reduce friction between these siblings.

Twins and Other Siblings
When Judy T. was three and a half years old, her mother had identical twin girls, Leslie and Laura. The advent of twins led to unexpected changes in the household and absorbed a lot more of their mother's time and energy than would otherwise have been the case. "Twins don't double your work," one mother points out. They quadruple it." In addition to all this, the twins had blue eyes and golden curly hair, while Judy's eyes were an ordinary brown and her hair straight and mousy—facts driven home to her by the unthinking remarks of friends and relatives:

"Aren't the twins absolutely adorable?"

"You must be *so* proud, dear, to have such beautiful sisters!"

"Isn't it too bad Judy has such plain straight hair, when the little dolls have those beautiful curls?"

Little wonder that Judy became moody and introverted. Coping with a new baby in the family is tough enough, but how can any young sibling cope with this kind of double trouble? The child's parents were sensitive to the problem and worked hard to bolster and support their firstborn, but it wasn't until Judy started nursery school—where she experienced a new and exciting setting, plus help from an understanding teacher—that she began coming out of her shell. Now Judy is eight years old, has achieved some solid psychological footing, is beginning at last to respond to her twin sisters, and is even beginning to take some pride in them. Judy helps her mother with the twins and looks forward to the day when she'll be old enough to be their baby-sitter.

Judy's initial reaction points up the fact that, for the other siblings, the presence of twins (or triplets) can be more than ordinarily traumatic. Not only do multiple-birth children seem to get more attention than a single child, but the multiple-borns have each other and can live in a kind of "closed society" that is fairly secure and comforting. Psychiatrist Herman Roiphe, of the Mount Sinai School of Medicine, explains that the challenge for a single sibling is "the fact that twins are somehow bound in exclusive closeness which locks everyone else out."

But this has certain benefits as far as sibling rivalry goes: Since twins have their own private dual-sufficiency, they aren't as likely to engage in excessive fighting with the other kids in the family. Starting off with status and prestige, having each other for company, twins have less need to test themselves against other siblings in a classic tug-cf-war for self-esteem.

Again, a lot depends on the youngsters' age spans, personalities, and how parents treat their children individually. In those cases where a single sibling is five or more years older than the twins, there's often a lot less jealousy and a lot more interest and pride. One teenage girl states that she never felt deprived after twin baby boys arrived in her family. On the contrary, she joined in the fuss over them and enjoyed it all. "Having them be unique," she recalls, "made me feel unique, too."

Where a sibling is younger than the twins, similar influences are at work. The youngest child of the family usually gets extra parental care and concern, but this isn't seen as a threat: Since they have each other, twins are less likely to be envious of attentions paid to a younger brother or sister.

Twins can also turn to each other for solace and protection against any taunting and teasing by their older siblings.

THE PARENT'S ROLE

For parents, the challenge here, as in any sibling situation, is to treat each child in the family as fairly as possible—and as an individual. Experts in child rearing at the Princeton Center for Infancy advise against giving twins cute names that rhyme. Nor, they say, should parents dress these youngsters exactly alike or expect them to share identical toys, friends, and so on. They also think it best to separate twins early in their school careers. Some authorities feel twins should be kept together at least through nursery school and kindergarten before separation is attempted. But the question has to be decided carefully because identical twins may need each other for security, and such separation can be too traumatic. In general, without negating the all-important bond, twins should be encouraged as far as possible to develop their own likes, dislikes, friends, abilities, and interests. Authorities at the Princeton Center for Infancy sum it up simply: "Parents should react to each child as a separate entity, and avoid viewing their twins as a set."

Parents of twins also have a special responsibility toward the single siblings in the family—to see that they aren't shortchanged when it comes to affection and that their lives aren't overshadowed by the excitement of a multiple birth. Once the immediate fuss and enthusiasm quiet down, attention—in fact, extra attention—can be paid to the other children, who now more than ever will need to know and feel that they are indeed loved, important members of the family circle.

CHAPTER
12

Other Constellations

When Walter and I got married, he had *his* two children, and I had *my* two—I really thought, now this is wonderful. This is going to be fine. We were so lonesome before; now we'll be one big happy family. Well, it was a nice fantasy, but it didn't *quite* work out that way!

We've been looking at sibling rivalry, up to this point, in terms of fairly conventional families, but in today's society there are many variations on the traditional family unit. The statistics tell it all. Currently, one child in six lives in a single-parent household. Our divorce and separation rate is soaring, and experts at the U.S. Census Bureau now estimate that some 40 percent of marriages among couples in their twenties will eventually end in divorce. In addition, over seven million young children are living with parents who have remarried—and while some of these are due to the death of an adult, the vast majority involve earlier marital breakups. Still other children are part of informal live-in arrangements, which may or may not be lasting.

All of this has resulted in a whole new kinship vocabulary. Today we're all familiar with such terms as *single parents, custodial parents, blended families, stepsiblings, half-siblings, natural parents, nonresident parents, live-ins,* and so on. The basic family constellation has gone through upheavals; as a result, both parents and children may find themselves in unexpected roles. And all of us are now aware that many family units today are not nuclear units, but are reconstituted and merged families based on the marriage-divorce-remarriage cycle.

Where people are concerned, new roles often involve new rules, and nowhere is this more apparent than in the area of sibling rivalry. While circumstances may change, a child's needs remain basically the same. Every child, regardless of family makeup, has a need for love, acceptance, and inner security, also a natural urge to strive, compete, and develop. But when circumstances do change, the needs may express themselves in new and different ways. Let's consider some of these changes and the challenges they offer.

SINGLE PARENTS AND SIBLING RIVALRY

Thomas L., a divorced father living in New York, says,

> Wendy and I split up a little over two years ago, when Jamie was five and Leslie was eight. Neither Wendy nor I have remarried as yet. The kids now live with their mother; I have them on alternate weekends and for part of every summer. We get along very well—I've always managed to stay close to them—but I noticed some subtle changes during that first year. The kids battled a good bit when we were all together and they still fight a lot; but after Wendy and I broke up, it seems to me that they vied more to get my attention. Maybe it was because they didn't see me as much, or whatever. But they did compete constantly to sit next to me, talk to me, and so on. It's tapered off some, but for a while it seemed very important for them to get me involved in all their activities.

Thomas's ex-wife has a parallel story, one that, among single parents, is fairly typical when children find they can no longer share both mother and father under one roof.

A number of studies reveal behavior changes among siblings in single-parent households, changes that are intense,

but often short-lived. Some newly divorced parents report
reactions similar to the one just cited. In these homes, rivalry
between siblings tends to intensify, especially in competing
for a parent's attention. It's almost as if each child, shaken by
the split, inevitably feeling less secure, works harder to acquire a bigger "piece" of the parent on the scene and is more
alert to any threat to those rights. So there may be, as in the
case of Jamie and Leslie, increased competition for the love
and approval of each individual parent.

In other cases, the opposite reaction takes place. Many
divorced parents report that, for a while at least, there is a
lessening of rivalry. Like Hansel and Gretel of fairytale fame,
huddled together for protection, these children establish a
kind of détente, joining forces and strengths to face a world
that suddenly appears unstable. Where adult discord prior to
the breakup was especially harsh, with loud and bitter arguments, this kind of sibling alliance is understandably more
intense. At such times, children may—and do—turn to each
other for a degree of stability and support, allowing their
own discords to fade.

Both these reactions—the increase or the lessening of rivalry—do, in most cases, tend to pass; it's well to remember
that the first few months are the hardest. Gradually, as new
arrangements are made, as life goes on, as kids realize that the
world hasn't ended after all, normalcy returns and with it the
healthy kind of competition that marks most sibling relationships. But there are a number of other factors that single
parents have to be aware of and guard against.

The "Adult Substitute" Syndrome

One tendency, noted in surveys, is for a single parent to
make an older child into a kind of substitute for the missing
adult. Understandably, when marriages break up, single parents will often turn to their children for companionship and
emotional support formerly provided by a mate. This is especially so with the parent who continues to live with the
children and retains custodial care. As one mother of a four-

teen-year-old son put it recently, "We're not equals exactly, but I probably regard him more as an equal than I would if I lived with another adult."

There is, in short, a natural tendency among singles to lean more on the children, especially the older ones, and to give them wider latitude and responsibility than they might have had otherwise. Where the custodial parent works outside the home, the teenager may be given a lot of responsibility in caring for younger siblings. Single parents may also expect their kids to help in making serious family decisions.

Asking youngsters suddenly to take on adult roles obviously places a heavy, sometimes unfair, burden on them. It aggravates sibling rivalry by giving older kids too much power and authority over the younger ones. Conversely, a teenager can resent feeling overwhelmed with duties and unable to enjoy the usual fun of childhood.

There are both advantages and disadvantages in giving kids added roles and responsibilities. If not carried to extreme, this approach does help youngsters toward maturity and encourages feelings of self-sufficiency and self-esteem. But a fine line has to be drawn, especially when it comes to decision making. The all-important guideline to keep in mind is to share decision making whenever it feels appropriate but not to turn it over to the children. The final decision must always rest with responsible parents.

The "Choose Up Sides" Syndrome
Subtler but more destructive is a tendency among some divorced parents to enlist the kids in what is clearly and strictly an adult battle. While most parents are knowledgeable and sensitive about this, there are still some cases where, out of bitterness and anger, single parents may expect the children to take sides in the marital dispute. Sometimes one parent will undercut the other or will use normal sibling competition to divide the kids into two separate camps. But children are neither adults nor pawns and should be spared these roles for the sake of their emotional health.

Of course, when adults feel bitter and hurt, it isn't easy to shield the children from these perfectly human reactions. But one safeguard is for the parents involved to find other outlets—friends, relatives, counselors—with whom they can safely talk out their feelings, thus ensuring that the kids won't be inadvertently used for that purpose.

In a similar way, children of divorce sometimes try to work one parent against the other, playing on the guilt and frustration of the adults to win advantages for themselves. Again, single parents must be on the alert for this kind of manipulation.

Carol O., divorced mother of three youngsters, recalls her own problems and reactions:

> John and I had a rough time during the breakup. There was a lot of bitterness—well, there still is—but we tried not to let it rub off on the kids. I never say anything bad or negative about John. He is their father; he's been a good parent, the kids love him, and I don't want to get in the way of that. I won't let the kids play games with me, either. I think they're aware of the hard feelings between John and me, and sometimes they try to take advantage, getting one of us to join their side against the other. But they really don't do it very much, because I won't go along with it.

Another divorced parent, father of two siblings, summed it up this way:

> I see my kids regularly, and we're very close; but sometimes they try to use their mother or myself as pawns. They do try, but it's something I feel strongly about. I don't want that sort of involvement unless it's some kind of really serious matter. My ex-wife and I have a good relationship—I guess what it is, is that we both trust each other. So if one of the kids came to me and said, "Mommy's not fair; she always favors Jennifer and she never believes my side," I really wouldn't want to hear that. I think what I would say is, "You'll need to find some way to say that directly to your mother." I would also

say, "If you want, I'll talk to your mother about it and tell her that this is the way you're feeling now, but wouldn't it be best if you told her?" Being kids, sure, they try to manipulate us. But I don't let them get away with it, because it's destructive to everyone.

What this tells us in effect is that kids are indeed consistent and will try to win their competitive goals in many ways, devious or otherwise. In general, once the trauma of separation is past, sibling rivalry in single households follows much the same course as it does in two-parent homes. Depending on the sex of the siblings and their age span, normal squabbling and bickering will go on. In single-parent families there are certainly new aspects to the rivalry and new complications, but all this is solvable where both of the parents involved are objective, honest, and fully aware of the real needs of their children.

STEPSIBLINGS AND STEPPARENTS

Cinderella, that paragon of patience and virtue, is one of the best known of all our fairy tale characters. Victimized by her cruel stepmother and mean stepsisters, she won out in the end, symbolizing the triumph of the helpless over the powerful. The same pattern is found in other fairy tales. Snow White's jealous stepmother (no longer "the fairest of them all") banishes her beautiful stepdaughter from the palace. And in Hansel and Gretel, a wicked stepmother persuades her doltish husband to abandon her stepchildren in the forest.

This myth of the cruel stepparent, present in many folk and fairy tales, is as persistent as it is unfair; as child psychologist Dr. Emily Visher points out, "Stepmothers have always had a bad press." But children's storybooks notwithstanding, modern stepmothers are a far cry from the kind who bullied the likes of Cinderella; and the myth of the heartless new spouse couldn't, in today's world, be further from the truth.

According to the U.S. Census Bureau, there are thirty-five million adults in America now living in stepfamily relationships. And due to the pattern of divorce and remarriage, over a thousand new stepfamilies with young children are being created everyday. In addition, there are many households where children share one parent and the parent's live-in companion, an arrangement closely paralleling remarriage. As all these adults struggle to build new lives and new family relationships, their experiences produce fresh insights into problems of child rearing and sibling rivalry. They also give us a greater understanding of the pitfalls and roadblocks along the way.

One Big, Happy Family
The stereotype of the cruel, unfeeling stepparent is and always has been largely unrealistic; sensitive, dedicated adults needn't take it too literally. Still there are some reactions that, though quite normal, can be harmful. After all, every stepchild is a real, live reminder of the spouse's previous marriage. This may well lead to adult feelings of jealousy, complicated by resentment of the time and attention the spouse devotes to his or her natural children. Such negative human feelings can be sensed intuitively by stepchildren, who may thus view the new parent as a "bad mommy" or a "bad daddy," especially when measured against the absent parent, who becomes highly idealized.

These suspicions and resentments do crop up and have to be dealt with. But there's another, more persistent matter that calls for our consideration. This is the myth of the "one big, happy family," an ideal and valued goal that is often reached more in fantasy than in fact.

"I don't have to listen to you—you're not my real father!"

"Mommy's new husband always sticks up for *his* kids, and never for *us*."

"Why do I have to love her or be nice to her? She isn't my real sister anyway."

Comments like these are only the tip of the stepfamily

iceberg, but they accent the difficulties that arise when adults remarry and bring their children from previous unions. Ideally everyone wants, and hopes for, harmony and happiness in the new family constellation. In reality—and this includes areas of sibling rivalry—unexpected stresses and strains can develop that have to be dealt with frankly, honestly, and at times with almost superhuman patience. As one harrassed mother says, "Bill and I wanted this marriage so much, we needed it so much, we really thought it would solve all our problems. Instead, we found a whole bunch of new problems, and we weren't prepared. We found that making a go of it took lots and lots of patience and hard work."

Building a stepfamily with solid, satisfying relationships is hard work certainly, but the end goals are attainable, and the process can be helped if certain principles are kept in mind.

Instant Love
First and foremost, there must be an acceptance of the fact that instant love is neither likely nor logical; to expect it to be is naive. If love isn't a cookie jar (see chapter 8), it isn't a light switch either, which can be clicked on or off at will. Affection, trust, warmth of feeling—all of these have to be nurtured gradually; they take time to grow and develop, *particularly among young stepsiblings*. After all, there's no real reason why the kids of one parent should feel instant, automatic affection for the kids of another. On the contrary, young children often greet these new combinations with anxiety, suspicion, and, in many cases, plain hostility.

This resentment and hostility may extend not just to the new stepparent (who is seen as usurping the role held by the natural parent) but to the children of the stepparent as well. When young siblings are thrust suddenly into a tidy, preset family unit, they can be looked on by the other kids as challengers and invaders. As a result, everyone's guard is up, and the way is paved for considerable friction. To a great degree, in the early stages of a new arrangement, this is only natural. To expect instant camaraderie between stepsiblings is unrealistic; they need time to shed their natural instincts of resentment or mistrust and to grow into trust and friendship.

New Combinations
In primary families—that is, with a natural mother and father both present—sibling rivalry is part of daily living and, within limits, it can have a strong, positive effect on a child's development. But in stepfamilies this rivalry may take more complicated forms. For example, where a young brother and sister live with a divorced mother, there will be a one-to-one rivalry pattern. When mother remarries and stepfather brings a new stepbrother and stepsister into the family, the rivalry combinations increase greatly.

Perhaps at first, the two sibling pairs will join together and compete as teams—"us" against "them." Later, depending on the ages of the kids, the two older stepsiblings may focus competitively on each other, or they may tend to unite against the younger ones. If one of the four kids in our sample family is particularly aggressive, he or she may try to dominate all three of the other sibs. Rivalry divisions may also form along sexual lines—the boys against the girls.

In primary families the closest relationships tend to be between sibs of the same sex; but recent research shows that in stepfamilies the closest bonding is often between the opposite sexes. Researcher Lucille Duberman theorizes that this may have a sexual basis: There can well be physical attraction between a stepsister and a stepbrother, but because of the family context, romance is taboo. Instead the two children, drawn instinctively toward each other, will develop a strong friendship, a bond that lasts throughout their adult lives.

Where stepmother and stepfather decide to have children of their own, still another dimension is added. Depending, again, on the age and temperaments of the stepsibs and the nature of the family relationships, this new member (or members) can have a divisive effect or—in many cases—provide an emotional tie that links all the siblings more closely. For instance, the older kids may be jealous and assume that the new baby will be more loved and valued than they themselves are. Conversely, a new child of both parents can confirm to them that the marriage is "real" and will not dissolve or magically disappear. In these cases, the new baby becomes a focus of good feelings, a new family member whom the other kids can share and enjoy equally.

But regardless of varying patterns and combinations, the basic nature of sibling squabbles remains largely unchanged. There will be plenty of competition for parental time, for possessions, for TV rights, for "the biggest piece of cake," and also the usual hurt feelings, complaints, and indignant cries of "it's not fair!" Dealing with all that poses a challenge for stepparents, but the guidelines already suggested in this book still apply. In time, stepsibling rivalry usually sorts itself out and simmers down to acceptable levels, but a lot depends on the fairness and patience of the adults involved and the ability of parents to be realistic in their expectations.

The Role of the Stepparent
Just as instant love is a fantasy ideal in stepfamilies, so, too, is the concept of *instant parent*. One father, recently remarried to a woman with children of her own, said, "I thought that being a good parent wasn't easy, but it's child's play compared with being a good stepparent."

It's important from the very beginning to recognize that stepparenting is different from primary parenting. For one thing, the role of stepparent is a much more self-conscious one than the role of parent: It's difficult for stepparents to behave spontaneously, since they are so constantly aware of being tested by friends, relatives, spouse, and the children themselves. The role of stepmother is perhaps the most difficult of all, since she often feels that her performance is being watched and judged. As a result, she must become a "supermom" in order to succeed.

Another reason for self-consciousness is that, in many cases, there's a natural parent hovering somewhere in the immediate background. Quite often the stepparent feels more like an extra parent than a substitute parent. This sense of being an "extra" can understandably have an inhibiting effect on how a stepparent deals with children's problems and behavior.

Marie S., mother of one child and stepmother of two others, says,

> I'm always so aware of the fact that Henry's children do have their own mother, whom they see quite a lot. Even though the kids live with us, I find that when I have to discipline one of my "steps" or yell at them, I can't be natural about it. I sort of hold back, almost as if I have no right to really play a mother role. I'm fond of my stepchildren, and they like me— but it would help a lot if I could feel more relaxed about it.

This inner tug-of-war puts an extra burden on a stepparent in handling sibling rivalry and similar problems. It's harder for a stepfather, for example, to break up a fight between his own child and a stepchild without risking an accusation of favoritism—and deep down this adult may indeed question his own motives. Conversely, this same parent, fearful of playing favorites, may be unduly harsh with his own kids while leaning over backward to be lenient and permissive with his stepchildren.

Dealing with, and overcoming, these dilemmas calls for patience and perseverance. There are no shortcuts or easy answers, but it can be done. Stepparents need to realize that theirs is indeed a special role, different from the role of natural parents. As a result, stepparents do have to work harder to win the kind of acceptance and approval of their stepchildren that natural parents simply take for granted. One stepmother, with many years of trial-and-error experience, sums it up:

> I'm *not* my stepchildren's real mother—I know it and they know it. But they also know that we have certain rules, simple rules, about living together in one household. Their father and I expect them to live up to these rules, and they expect me

to treat them fairly. And we've found that when we cooperate honestly with one another, it works out fine.

USING LITERATURE

Just as there are books that can help a young child prepare for the arrival of a new baby, there are excellent books today designed to help older children adapt to living in stepfamilies. Here is a listing of some recommended volumes with brief content descriptions that stepsiblings can benefit from as well as enjoy reading:

Stepchild by Terry Berge (Julian Messner).

Nine-year-old David tells, in the first person, about living with his mother and new stepfather and having to relate to his stepfather's two children, whom David calls the "steps." Initial hostility and resentment gradually give way to positive feelings in this sensitive story, told in photographs.

My Other-Father, My Other-Mother by Harriet Langstrom Sobol (Macmillan).

In this photo-illustrated story, eleven-year-old Andrea talks about her "complicated" family life. She and her brother live with their mother and new stepfather and often visit their natural father, who has also remarried. Andrea, despite minor difficulties, likes both of her new stepparents. A warm, upbeat approach to stepfamilies, without excessive soul-searching.

The Animal, the Vegetable, and John D. Jones by Betsy Byars (Delacorte).

Two young girls, Clara and Deanie, are spending the summer at the shore with their divorced father and his live-in friend, who has her son with her. There is instant enmity between the youngsters, but a near tragedy for Clara gives the kids a new perspective. They begin to see things differently and start to feel some sense of real kinship.

Maybe It Will Rain Tomorrow by Jane Breskin Zalben (Farrar, Straus, Giroux).

Beth Corey hates living with her father, his new wife, and their new baby, but now that her mother is dead, she has nowhere else to go. A summer romance helps Beth to understand the value of needing and sharing, and the young woman slowly begins to learn how to accept and enjoy her new stepfamily.

Footsteps on the Stairs by C. S. Adler (Delacorte).

Two young teenage stepsisters share a vacation at an old beach house that turns out to be haunted. The girls start out with hostility toward each other, but learn something about give-and-take when they encounter spooky sisters from the past. An unusual ghost story with a happy ending.

For younger children:

All Kinds of Families by Nora Simon (Albert Whitman).

A sensitive view, with charming illustrations, of the real meaning of families and family bonding. Without focusing specifically on stepfamilies, a basic message of comfort and love comes through to young readers: Families come in different shapes and sizes and are made up of people who live, love, work, fight, play, and share together—and truly care about one another.

CHAPTER 13

"... *Boy, It's Great When It Works"*: *One Stepmother's Story*

Nancy M. had been married five years, with two small children, when her world suddenly caved in. Out of the blue, her husband suddenly announced that there was "someone else" and that he wanted a divorce.

Several years later, Nancy met and married her present husband, Alan, who had two children of his own—twin boys age seven. At that time the twins were living with Alan's ex-wife. Later she gave up custody, and they came to live with Alan, Nancy, and Nancy's children.

The problems, pitfalls—and eventual triumphs—of this couple reflect the experiences of many stepparents. They are well described in Nancy M.'s lively comments:

"We gained final custody of Alan's twins in 1975, at which time they were nine, and my children were four and six. And by then, Alan and I had our own child, a little girl, who was just a baby. That's our background. The twins are now almost grown; my kids are fifteen and thirteen, and Sally—that's the 'ours'—is eight. So we have quite an array here! Quite a family. It really turned out well, but believe me, there were times when I thought it never would.

"Now, this is kind of important. I'm not a trained psychologist or anything like that—I've just *lived* it all—and I can make one flat statement: It has been a lot of work. But I do find nowadays that our stepchildren get along with our natural children just as well as our natural children get along with each other. Maybe even better. They have a relationship that I'd certainly call normal in every way. They're quick to criticize each other; they're also quick to defend each other. They speak of each other as 'my sister' and 'my brother.' They call each other bad names and good names. And they don't make distinctions as far as being 'steps.' But they've had nine years to grow together.

"At first it was very rough. You have to remember that these two sets of kids, mine and Alan's, were coming together from their own little families, and there was a lot of anxiety and insecurity about having to leave one parent. Adults may not see that right away; we only see our own problems without realizing that these children have problems, too. They have just left a parent, and they wonder why.

"So stepchildren come into a new family with the aggression already there. They want to fight. They want to argue. They want some answers. They come to the new parent with a good deal of anger and hostility. As I look back, I can see that this was normal, though at the time I was very upset. I thought when Alan's twins came to live with us, we would all love each other instantly. I would love them just as I loved my own—if necessary, I'd force my love on them. Not very realistic. Actually, deep down I was resentful and jealous, because the twins represented Alan's earlier life and relationship.

"The boys also meant more work for me. Looking at myself ten years back, I think I was selfish, but I didn't know it then. Because there was so much more work, I probably put some of my prejudice against the twins onto my own kids. So some of the sibling fights probably arose because they saw that their own mother resented these newcomers. Also, a stepmother has a lot of extra pressures because of her role as nurturer. I felt that pressure, and if it hadn't been for Alan—

who is a marvelous person and who understood what was going on—I don't think I would have made it through this.

"Now something sticks out in my mind so vividly: the first time we were all together—and I think that it points up the aggressiveness and the rivalry and the jealousy. The twins hadn't been in the house for more than two hours. It was the week after Christmas. They went down into the basement, got Alan's golf clubs, and completely demolished a new racing car that my son had gotten from him. One of those plastic cars you get in and pedal.

"Talk about strong emotions! The boys were just overwhelmed; they resented me, they resented my children, they resented their father being there, and resented the racing car. Before this they'd really been neglected by their mother, badly neglected, and suddenly it was all too much for them.

"Well, that was the start, and when I realized that we were going to have to live together—I guess it was normal that I got very depressed. It took effort and a lot of patience on my husband's part; it took a lot of crying and a lot of depression. But it also took pulling ourselves up and saying, 'Hey, these kids have been through a lot; we can't let them go through any more. We parents are going to have to stop playing these games. I'm going to have to try to stop being supermom; I'm going to have to relax; I'm going to have to stop forcing myself upon them. I'm going to have to accept them as members of the family on equal ground, and let's just see what happens.' And we have pulled together gradually over nine years, and now it is marvelous, because it works. And you know, Sally helped a lot—the child that's Alan's and mine.

"Sally is a wonderful buffer. I must boast about her because she gets most of her qualities from my husband. She has this emotional stability. I'm a very emotional person; Alan is very calm. And as I said, we couldn't have made it without his steadiness, his anchoring. Sally, thank heavens, inherited my freckles and eyes, and Alan's emotional stability! She was also a signal to the other kids that Alan and I were for real, that we were sticking together. This, I think, is what Sally represented. Remember, this was early in our marriage, and there was still a lot of enmity between the stepsiblings. As long as Alan and I didn't have a child, the factions could pair off: Mom had her two, Dad had his two—and I suspect the kids thought, 'We can still pull them apart. Then we'll get things back to where they were.'

"But Sally, as I say, was a symbol that a family was really starting. Symbols are important. The message that got through was, I think, 'This family is here to stay, and you're welcome to join us. But if you two factions continue to fight, it won't change a thing; that's your problem.' It did have an effect. Also, you see, the baby represented half of each side, so in a way, they each owned half of Sally. I think they even said at the time—in their own words—that they each owned half of Sally.

"We also bought a larger house then, and that was symbolic, too. Instead of everybody being crammed into my old house, sharing rooms, being uncomfortable, suddenly we were making a fresh start. Everyone had their own rightful place and room for their own things and so on. So the symbolism of Sally and the new house helped a lot here. . . .

"Well, we've been married ten years and we can laugh about our past lives, as we call them. With the kids, the changes have really been something. Now, whether they're just being polite to each other, I don't know. But that's fine. If they want to sweep their battles under the rug, that's better than rockin' and sockin'! Also, I see my oldest girl, Laurie, getting along better with the twins than with her natural brother. I guess what I'm trying to say is that I don't see any real differences now—there's no 'choosing up sides.' They're just normal sibs interacting well with each other.

"Again, I think an awful lot depends on the parents. With stepsiblings, it seems to be more of an adult problem than it is with natural siblings. I think when parents stop playing games with their ex's and stop playing games with the kids, it can work. Parents who remarry tend to play games, so the children and stepchildren kind of react the way the parents are programming them. But when this stops, and when the steppar.nts don't try to do anything special for the step-children that they wouldn't do for their own children—when they start to treat them all equally—then, I think, the kids get the idea, 'Hey, maybe I *am* a member of this family.' But I will not say that anyone can get to the place where we are now without going through this business I've just described; I don't think it's possible, just because of the emotions. You've got to work through your emotions, and it takes time.

"I would be very surprised if anyone can get married, bring in the stepchildren, and have instant success. It just does not happen that way. Aside from setting rules and reg-ulations for the kids, Alan and I had to work through our emotions before we could even start on the children. For instance, as a stepmother, you bend over backward for your husband's children because you don't feel the same quality of love for them as you do for your own children. So you're trying to compensate, trying to force it. Also, you're over-reacting to protect your own kids; it's your maternal instinct.

"Most of Alan's and my arguments revolved around the children. Usually it was my opinion about what his kids were doing wrong, while I ignored what role my own kids may have been playing. Parents do have to deal with their own jealousy and their protective feelings toward their own kids. We didn't let the problems destroy us, though, because we saw that they could. They could get out of hand, and that would serve no purpose but to throw the kids right back into misery and confusion. And so we had to grow up. Had to get hold of our emotions and not be afraid to talk everything out. Everything. We set up certain ideals for ourselves and tried to follow them. Sometimes we did, sometimes we didn't. It wasn't easy, but we kept at it. I don't know if this means anything, but we feel secure enough in our family, in our interrelations, that we're taking in a foreign-exchange stu-dent this fall! We feel good enough about each other that we can invite this young student, a total stranger, to join our family. And we're all looking forward to it.

"When something like this works, boy, is it rewarding. You feel like you've really accomplished something. I don't want to sound smug or come off as bragging—but you really have done something: You've taken two different sets of children in what really could have been a disaster—and there are a lot of kids in this world, unfortunately, who are living in disasters—you've taken them and, through a lot of hard work, given them a normal family life and a home with real sisters and brothers, and we're proud of that. . . .

"What advice would I give to someone about to enter a situation similar to ours? I would say, 'Hey, do it. It's not going to be easy; it's going to be an emotional roller coaster—but boy, it's great when it works. And you've done what you could to give emotional stability to children who may not have had emotional stability otherwise. So just do it, because it's worth it!'"

CHAPTER
14

Adding It Up

Home is the place where we create the future—the place
where children are prepared to grow toward independence
and a way of living in the wider world. Home is a launching
platform, and families set the launching process in motion.
—Dr. T. Berry Brazelton

It's only in the past few decades that sibling rivalry has, in a
sense, been "discovered." Of course siblings and their conflicts have always been a well-known part of the family picture, but only in recent years has this rivalry been seen in a
new light. Educators and child psychologists now recognize
that this rivalry isn't just a trivial annoyance, but plays a truly
important part in a child's growth, development, and personality. At the same time, we have learned that kids are
influenced not only by the actions of their parents, but perhaps even more by the actions of the other sibs in the family
constellation.

We know now that sibling rivalry, within limits, is healthy
and natural, and literally helps children to chart their paths
through the early years of self-discovery. We also know that,
along with the battling and squabbling, there's a good deal of
affiliation and bonding: Sibs may fight heartily at home, but
let an outsider try to interfere and the sibs will band to-

gether for defense and mutual protection. As children grow into adults, this supportive side of the relationship often comes to the fore; brothers and sisters who fought like cats and dogs as children may indeed become warm and devoted friends in later years.

We know, too, that the sibling relationship is a subtle mix of many childhood drives and motives; these include jealousy, competition, the testing of parents, the testing of self, and the struggle for power. How can modern parents successfully deal with so complex a process? There are no easy answers, but fortunately there are few insoluble problems. In some cases—a tiny minority—where rivalry is violent and vicious, or deteriorates into hatred, outside help will be needed; in these situations, parents shouldn't hesitate to talk to family counselors or other professionals. Counseling also helps where parents feel helpless, confused, unable to cope with their own anger, or unable to judge whether the squabbling is normal or not. In the great majority of families, however, sibling conflicts do follow a fairly normal day-to-day pattern as the kids fight, make up, play happily together—then start scrapping all over again.

Is all this easy for parents to live with? At times, certainly not. As one mother says, "There are some days when I feel I need nerves of steel, the wisdom of Solomon, and a good pair of earmuffs." But it does help if we can accept the fact that much of this behavior is in actuality a necessary part of sibling growing pains.

Throughout these pages, various guidelines have been given to help parents understand and deal with sibling conflicts. At this point, let's review some of the more important of these suggestions:

· When brothers and sisters bicker and squabble, they are engaging in perfectly natural, ritualized behavior. It's normal for siblings to compete. Rivalry helps them to learn about themselves and to test their strengths and weaknesses.
· Don't always look for, or expect to find, logical "reasons"

for squabbling. A good deal of sibling rivalry is instinctive and is based on inner psychological drives. When two sibs squabble over a magazine or a cookie, it's not the object as such that really matters. That magazine or that cookie often symbolizes a child's hunger to acquire his or her "fair share in life."

· Underlying many surface squabbles is the sibling's deep, intense need for parental love and attention—an important reason why parents should lavish their affection as much as possible on each child as a *unique individual*.

· In most cases, it's best for parents to stay out of sibling arguments: When kids work through their own squabbles and settle their quarrels by themselves, they gain confidence and self-reliance. And this, of course, helps to prepare them for the competitive society they'll face as adults.

· One clear exception to the noninterference rule is in the case of violence. Parents should tolerate no violence, either physical or verbal, among their siblings. This rule should be established early and enforced firmly.

· Inevitably, parents will be called on at times to act as referees and to settle disputes. Where a parental decision does have to be made, keep it simple and as fair as possible. But a parent should also remember that it's impossible to please everyone. There's no such thing as being one hundred percent fair all the time, in every situation.

· Parents should avoid a pattern of making comparisons between their children. A comparison is a judgment; both sides usually lose, and no sibling has ever changed his or her behavior in order to "be just like" a favored sister or brother.

· Having to share is important—but so is not having to share. Possessions give kids a sense of personal identity. Every sib has a right to his or her very own possessions and a proper place to keep them. And these rights should be respected by all the members of the family.

· The arrival of a new baby is bound to be stressful for the older child or children. While baby's needs obviously are very urgent, this shouldn't signal neglect or indifference to the needs of the other siblings—emotional as well as physical.

- Age, sex, and birth order all play a part in child development. No two kids are ever born into exactly the same family and no two kids develop and grow at exactly the same pace—facts to keep in mind when evaluating your siblings or pushing them to live up to your expectations.
- A stepparent often faces greater emotional pressure than a natural parent, because the role is a self-conscious one. Stepparents have to guard against instinctively favoring or protecting their own children; conversely, they shouldn't lean over backward, favoring the stepchildren to show how "impartial" they are. The truly fair approach is to treat each child honestly—and according to his or her *individual* needs and nature.
- In dealing with siblings and sibling rivalry, it's important to keep in mind that parental love is not a fixed quantity or a substance that can be doled out in measured amounts, spoonful by spoonful. Each child is indeed unique and needs to feel his or her own individuality. "Fairness" and "sameness" are not always identical; each unique child has his or her own different needs.

THE FINAL SAY

Direct experience is often the best teacher. Many parents have been interviewed for this book and have been quoted in its pages. These fathers and mothers have all dealt with siblings in their own families, and a few verbatim comments from them, and others, are worth reviewing:

"Sometimes when the kids start to fight, they'll come to us to settle it. Arguing about who picks TV shows, for instance. When we can, we toss the ball back to them. We'll spell out just what the problem is, and then the kids are asked to come up with solutions. We let them figure it out. They're much more committed to solutions they've thought up themselves."

"Our younger child was always more physical, more aggressive than the older one. Sometimes an older child has really to be protected from the younger one, who hasn't got the moral judgment—who just doesn't realize that you don't kick somebody in the wrong place or that you don't walk all over their things or suddenly attack them. The little ones need protecting—but at times the older siblings do, too."

"The most important thing to us was this business of letting our kids say what they felt. And not to be afraid to say it to us. I just can't emphasize that enough. No violence—that was definitely *out*—but they could put it into words. We feel pretty triumphant now, because we were going against the advice of some people who really thought our kids got along horribly. But it works fine. It cleared the air and saved us a lot of hassles."

"All kids aren't the same. I believe that children are born with a personality. And I think it's the task of parents to understand that personality and try to deal with it. The personality is there—it's a given—and I do think it's important to keep in mind."

"Susan and I are very conscious of balancing family time. We try to spend time as much as possible with each of our children alone. It's nothing rigid, you can't be rigid about it—but I guess we have a meter inside us; and every few days or weeks, we'll have a sense that we haven't had a special day with one or the other. Then we arrange something. As I say, it's not on a schedule, but we're very aware of that. The kids really need it, and so do we."

"Kids use language differently than adults do. It can be crude and pretty ugly, but it's on a different level. Children aren't affected by it in the same way adults would be."

"When our daughter was born, our two boys were then old enough to be somewhat trustworthy—if I was in the room—and to help me in many ways that a toddler couldn't have done—really to help. Did I let them? Absolutely, when they were around. But they both had such full lives of their own that they were not around a lot."

"Another system in our family is that things aren't always 'fair.' We've never told our kids that life is one hundred percent fair. In fact, sometimes when I say that they're not being fair to me, they say, "Aha! Life is not fair, Mommy!" But I've said to my son, when he complains about his little sister, 'At different stages in your life you get different privileges. Look, you get to stay up—she has to go to bed; you get to go out and spend the night with a friend—she's at home; you can ride a two-wheeler—she can't; now she sits in the front seat of the car where I can watch her—and you don't. It's just that at different times in your life, you do different things.'"

"I don't love all my children the same. I love my three children very much, but in different ways, and I do different things with them. Not always the same with each. I don't know how to say this exactly—I love them equally but differently. It can't be measured; it's a qualitative thing."

"In some families there is often some child who's just more gifted in many more areas than another child: socially, personally, in school, physical ability, so on. While I feel that competition is important and healthy, if it becomes a pattern where one is always losing in that competition, in that rivalry, then it becomes terribly painful to watch. Without neglecting the winners, I think parents have to make a special effort with the losers—spend more time with them, compliment them, help them to boost their self-esteem."

"I think that the new research is beginning to look at sisters and brothers, as well as at parents. Traditionally in psychology, the influence has been seen as coming from the top down, from the authority figures, and not as a two-way street. It wasn't understood for years that what the kids did affected the parents, just as what the parents did affected the kids. Now it's being seen as more complicated than people thought: The fact that what everyone in the family does affects everyone else. They are thinking much more these days in terms of networks instead of separate units."

Today's family constellations, like modern computer games, are indeed networks of complex interacting channels. Yet each network is rooted firmly in a home, and the feelings and attitudes prevalent in that home invariably affect all its members.

Each family sets its own individual tone and has its own problems, needs, and special concerns. But one thing that's shared by all of us is a need to live together and to interact with others in the same household. Home is the place where we help to create our children's future. And the quality of our love, our tact, and our understanding can do a lot toward making this future more viable, more fulfilling, more successful.

Recommended Reading

Elsewhere in these pages, certain books have been suggested that can help parents and siblings in dealing with specific aspects of this complex, intriguing subject.

For those parents who wish to pursue general areas of child care and child development, here is an additional list of recommended literature:

Between Parent and Child by Dr. Haim G. Ginott. Macmillan Co., New York, 1965.

The Sibling by Brian Sutton-Smith and B. G. Rosenberg. Holt, Rinehart and Winston, New York, 1970.

Toddlers and Parents by Dr. T. Berry Brazelton. Delacorte Press, New York, 1974.

The Parenting Advisor edited by Frank Caplan, Princeton Center for Infancy. Doubleday & Co., New York, 1977.

The Father's Almanac by S. Adams Sullivan. Doubleday & Co., New York, 1980.

What Every Child Needs by Lillian and Richard Peairs. Harper & Row, New York, 1974.

Between Generations by Ellen Galinsky. Berkley Books, New York, 1982.

Total Child Care by Lorian and Robert DeLorenzo. Doubleday & Co., New York, 1982.

Parents' Guide to Everyday Problems of Boys and Girls by Sidonie M. Gruenberg. Random House, New York, 1958.

The Magic Years by Selma H. Fraiberg. Scribners' Sons, New York, 1959.

Child Behavior by Drs. Ilg, Ames, and Baker, Gesell Institute of Human Development. Harper & Row, New York, 1981.

The Parents' Encyclopedia by M. I. Levine and J. H. Seligmann. Harper & Row, New York, 1978.

Joy in Parenting by Joy Schlehoffer. Paulist Press, New York, 1978.

The Pleasure of Their Company by Hooks, Boegehold, and Reit, Bank Street College of Education. Chilton Books, Pennsylvania, 1981.

The Complete Book of Sibling Rivalry by Dr. John McDermott. Wideview Books, New Jersey, 1980.

Making It As a Stepparent by Claire Berman. Doubleday, New York, 1980.

Raising Children in a Difficult Time by Dr. Benjamin Spock. Pantheon, New York, 1976.

Index

Printed in the United States
by Baker & Taylor Publisher Services